Soap Maker's Workshop

The Art and Craft of Natural Handmade Soap

©2010 Dr. Robert S. and Katherine J. McDaniel

Published by

kp **krause publications**

A division of F+W Media, Inc.

700 East State Street • Iola, WI 54990-0001
715-445-2214 • 888-457-2873
www.krausebooks.com

To order books or other products call toll-free 1-800-258-0929
or visit us online at www.krausebooks.com or www.Shop.Collect.com

Neither the authors nor Krause Publications are responsible for metric conversions.
All numbers are approximate.

Library of Congress Control Number: 2009937528

ISBN-13: 978-1-4402-0791-4
ISBN-10: 1-4402-0791-7

Cover Design by: Heidi Bittner-Zastrow
Designed by: Katrina Newby
Edited by: Candy Wiza
Photographers: Robert S. and Katherine J. McDaniel and Kris Kandler
Illustrator: Justin Lippert
Videographer: Kirsten Zastrow

Printed in China

Mission Statement: *Enjoy the simple things in life while you reduce, reuse and recycle.*

Make the change to a sustainable lifestyle using expert advice and know-how garnered from our Simple Living books. We'll provide you with the knowledge to develop long-term self-sufficiency through traditional skills, energy-efficient technology and eco-friendly environmental applications with step-by-step instructions that will save you time and money.

ACKNOWLEDGMENTS

Many people encouraged us and offered moral support and laughter
… mostly laughter, which is so important.

- Butch, Tamara, Lori, Melody, Amber, Pam and Trina, for their continued support, information and suggestions.

- Peter Nitschke, for being the best darn lawyer, fastest stick and "adopted son" on the face of the earth.

- Paul, Nancy and Tim, Sara and David, Ray and Carmen, Scotty and Bobby, Darien, Nick and Noel, Faye, Don, Bud, all the Carols but one, Corny, Buzz, Annette, Didibird, Rommel and Max, Lou, Joe and Luisito.

- Kathy Tarbox, publisher of the online soap- and candle-focused magazine, Saponifier, who allowed us free access to part or all of the many articles Bob wrote for Saponifier.

- Joe and Carol Ann and the Tartans of St. Margaret's Episcopal School, for sharing their space.

- Dlaura Loughrey, for taking the best photograph of us as a couple in our 40 years together.

— Bob and Katie McDaniel

CONTENTS

— Introduction —
BEGINNING THE ADVENTURE

We can hardly believe that "Essentially Soap" was published nearly 10 years ago. That book was roughly three years in the writing and represented not only the on-the-job expertise gained working for nearly 20 years in the soap and detergent and allied industries, but the evolution of thought and practice that comes from shifting from a manufacturing environment to a limited production of boutique soaps in a home lab or kitchen.

Writing "Essentially Soap" was hard work but we had fun selling our products at fine craft venues throughout the Northeast. We worked Winterthur (the DuPont estate in Delaware), helped launch the Kalmar Nyckel (a Swedish tall ship of the revolutionary war era) worked venues such as Franklin & Marshall and smaller venues in Pennsylvania, New Jersey and New York. These shows were invaluable. They enabled us to meet our public on a regular basis and learn what

people really liked and appreciated.

It is one thing to know the theory and chemistry of soap making, but whether we are hobbyists or small-businessmen, we don't just aim to please — we *have* to please. We have to be in touch with the times and the market. In our lifetime, public preference changed from all natural (which actually was the only thing available), to totally embracing new and improved synthetic products and finally returning to natural and sustainable. It has not been an easy journey, but it has always been interesting.

We bought into "better things for better living through chemistry." In the '50s it seemed so true that progress was marked by the addition of synthetic products designed in conjunction with Madison Avenue types who sold "new" as the measure of progress. Then the petroleum bubble started to burst and we realized that there was real value in wholesomeness and sustainability. We also realized that we were capable of transforming basic products into high-value items by applying our brains.

Soap making requires expertise, creativity, caution and a sense of fun and adventure. If you are reading this, you obviously have all the qualifications. Perhaps you are just starting out and planning to make a few bars for gifts or donations to fundraising events. Or maybe you're planning to join the hundreds and thousands in the soap cottage industry with plans to expand beyond the limits of your home to a sustainable business occupying thousands of square feet and employing numbers of people. It has been done before, and you can do it as well if you hone your expertise. Even experienced professionals learn new tricks, new tools, and even new insights into the process.

We have tried to incorporate the best practices into this book. Our emphasis has shifted to incorporate new techniques, new materials and new products with traditional expertise. We acknowledge that the market

has shifted to a new reality. Old is still good. Sustainable and natural is even better. And "green" means more than just a color — it is becoming a preferred lifestyle.

Once more we got excited as we prepared the multitude of samples to illustrate techniques and results. Soap making is a science, it is chemistry, it is an experience, which forces us to look at what we are doing and learn from each and every batch. Soap making is also an art. Bob's grandmother didn't consider herself a scientist as she made the soft soap that cleaned the family laundry. But what she did incorporated the same skills and art as making a fluffy biscuit. Some discoveries are incremental and some seem like vast revelations. "Soap Maker's Workshop" is our attempt to be there with you on your journey. You can read the complete book and try it all, one recipe at a time. You can skim through it until you find a section that looks really interesting and makes you itch to try it out. And, if you are experienced, you may find a new technique or insight into the chemistry. Whatever your skill level, read the safety instructions before starting.

We do have to warn you — soap making is habit forming! It appeals to those who want to use their hands to create something new; it appeals to those who want or need a home-based enterprise, which will enable them to stay home and still find a market to generate income. Hobbyists, small businesses and those expanding their markets — dive in. Join a chat list online; subscribe to an e-magazine, such as the Saponifier, which features soap making; join the Handcrafted Soapmakers Guild; read a book and get a new idea. Don't hesitate — go for it. We'll be here with you and so will our grandmothers.

Chapter One

FROM YESTERDAY TO TODAY: THE EVOLUTION OF SOAP

The urge to clean seems to be as old as civilization. Although, the earliest substances were not true soaps, but components (today called saponins) isolated from various plant sources. Initial usage probably was accidental, grabbing a handful of a saponin-containing plant along with the laundry at the edge of a stream. It wouldn't have taken much to realize that clothes didn't have to be pounded on the rocks quite so long whenever these plants were nearby.

THE EARLY YEARS

In primitive locations, soapwort or soaproot still is mashed up with water to produce a sudsy cleaning solution. Modern science still has not identified a milder cleanser for ancient tapestries than the soapwort that was used when the fabric was newly made. (Of course, today ancient tapestries are more likely to be carefully cleaned using a toothbrush instead of the traditional rocks.) Whatever the origin of soap, the first documented uses were certainly not for personal hygiene, but were for cleaning and processing hides and fleece. Practical soap making can be found mentioned on Sumarian clay tablets dating back to roughly 2500 B.C. The soap was produced from goat tallow and the lye processed from the ashes of a native bush. The soap was used to clean wool.

In any event, by first-century Rome, dye-containing soaps were used on hair (this fashion was borrowed from the Gauls), if not on other parts of the body. According to one charming legend (completely unsupported by any hard evidence), the word "soap" purportedly is derived from Mount Sapo, a place where animals were burned in sacrifice to the gods, a common practice in ancient Rome.

Rainwater naturally combined with the ashes from the altar, leaching out lye, which combined and reacted with residual animal fat rendered by the heat from the fire. Together they trickled down the hill (forming soap as they went) into the river Tiber. Ordinary Romans found that their clothes washed cleaner in the sudsy water near the altars. And when you are beating your clothing on river rocks, getting them cleaner faster is important and noteworthy.

Another school of thought argues that soap making was Celtic (or from the Berbers in North Africa) in origin and brought back to Rome with the conquering legions and their spoils. Since anything non-Roman was considered barbaric, a legend conveniently was concocted demonstrating the Roman-ness of the invention of soap. Although the conflicting theories of the discovery of soap have not been sorted out, by the time Vesuvius erupted in 79 A.D., destroying Pompeii and Herculaneum, a soap factory was among the industries that were encapsulated for posterity by the ash. It is perhaps fitting then that the Roman poet Pliny the Younger, who is often considered the inventor of soap around 77 A.D., was among the surviving witnesses to the destruction of Pompeii.

In a process related to traditional soap making, and one much less often mentioned, the Roman felt-makers (fullones) used a form of soap to clean hides and fleece. In this industry, one lucky employee

No matter who can claim credit for the invention of soap, the English word soap does in fact come from the Latin word for fat or grease. Which suggests that the Romans gloried in soapy bubbles in the public baths of the time — from the Eternal City to Britain. But, it is just not true. As a matter of fact, even though Romans may have made and used soap for the laundry and various industries, they did not value soap for cleaning people. For personal hygiene, olive oil was massaged into the body together with fine sand and, for the wealthy, slaves wiped off the dirty oil with a squeegee-like device called a strigil. After this, a plunge into the public baths rinsed off the residue.

got to visit the inns at the various crossroads and collect urine in crocks.

This was brought back to the workshop where it was poured into a shallow pit. Raw hides or fleece were then placed into the pit and another lucky employee got to hike up his toga, remove his sandals (hopefully) and spend the day walking over the hides and fleece in the pit. Of course, he was actually making soap, bringing the residual fat from the hides or the fatty lanolin from the fleece into contact with the ammonia from the urine, stirring it with his walking and heating it with the hot Roman sun. In this way, the excess fat was removed, the process of felting was begun and hides were softened and prepared for removing the residual hairs in the production of leather and parchments. This industry was odoriferous, though extremely profitable, and understandably often gave rise to complaints from the neighbors. However, the emperor eventually taxed these prosperous merchants and Emperor Vespasian is cited as referring to them by stating, *"pecunia non olet"* or "money does not smell."

The Romans may not be able to claim the invention of soap, but their growing empire certainly began to spread the use and production of soap throughout the "civilized" world of Europe and into Africa. By the eighth century, soap making was common in Italy and Spain. In the 13th century, soap was introduced in France, where soap was commonly made from goat tallow and alkali (lye) from beech ash.

FRENCH CONTRIBUTIONS TO SOAP MAKING

Over the next century or two, the French devised a method of making soap from olive oil rather than animal fat, producing Castile soap, a far milder soap than previously known. The French made at least three more key contributions to the development of soap making. It was the French who learned to make perfumed soap through the floral infusion of fat. *Enfleurage*, as it is known, is a multi-step process where fat is spread on a plank and then flowers or herbs are embedded into the fat, leading to the extraction of the natural fragrance oil from the flowers into the fat.

The process can be repeated several times to develop the desired fragrance intensity. The scented fat then can be used in the production of scented soap or processed further (extracted into alcohol) to isolate the floral oils for use in perfumery.

No doubt the French would have dominated the world soap industry except for two things: "luxury" soaps (really meaning all soap designed for personal use) were a common target for royal taxes, which put most soap out of the reach of commoners; more importantly, in the mid-14th century, personal bathing came to be considered highly dangerous.

Flowers and herbs are embedded into fat and pressed together with planks.

In the 1350s, the Black Death plague was pandemic. Of unknown origin, this invariably fatal disease was thought to have spread by noxious vapors, especially at night, and people who were damp from bathing were feared to be especially susceptible to catching this and other diseases. Although we know today that fleas carried by rats spread the plague, everyday life in European cities changed dramatically. Bathing became perhaps an annual event; windows, especially at night, were never opened; and in general, personal hygiene suffered in favor of masking the odors with perfumes, scented handkerchiefs, floral and herbal bouquets, and the like. In fact, in the 1600s there is a report of four French thieves who were caught robbing the bodies of plague victims. The automatic sentence of death was not carried out when they disclosed that they avoided the plague by using an herbal concoction of absinthe, rosemary, sage, peppermint, rue, lavender, calamus, cinnamon, clove, nutmeg and garlic all macerated together in vinegar with a bit of camphor.

THE AMERICAN COLONIES

In the early American colonies, most soap was made at home by boiling rendered animal fat with the alkali solution produced by treating hardwood ash with rainwater. Wood ash was a common source of sodium, and especially potassium hydroxides and carbonates, all forms of alkali. Rainwater was allowed to trickle through ashes, leaching out this lye mixture. A raw egg was often used to estimate the lye concentration: if the egg fell quickly through the lye, it was too weak and the solution was put back through the ashes to leach more alkali. If the egg floated on top, the lye was too concentrated and additional rainwater was added. If a more precise measure was desired, the concentration would be adjusted between batches so that the egg floated below the surface at

CREATING A LYE SOLUTION

A base of sand keeps ash and other solid impurities out of the lye.

Rain or other soft water is added and allowed to sit with the ash for about 24 hours to leach out the lye.

The lye solution, filtered by the sand layer, trickles from the bucket.

TESTING LYE SOLUTION

Floating an egg tests the strength of the lye. If the egg sinks, the lye solution is weak and it should be added to more ash to make a more concentrated solution.

When the egg floats at the top, the lye is strong enough for soap making.

The characteristic yellow color resulted both from color leached from the ashes and some rust from the cast-iron cooking pots generally used for soap making.

a constant depth from batch to batch. Proportions were determined by observation on the hardness of the soap or by tasting the product to see that excess lye (which tingled on the tongue) was not present.

The soap produced by this method was a soft soap, usually stored in kegs. When the soap maker wanted bar soap, she put the soap back in the kettle, boiled off more water and added handfuls of salt, which converted some of the softer potassium soap into the hard sodium form. As you can see, soap making was more an art than a science at that time, and often the balance between lye and fat was not quite right, resulting in a harsh soap that was great for the laundry and kitchen floor, but left something to be desired when used on face, hands and hair.

THE INVENTION OF SODA ASH

The second key French contribution, and the most critical advance in soap making, occurred in 1791 when the French chemist, LeBlanc, invented a process to make sodium carbonate — soda ash — from salt by an electrolytic reaction. Lye then could be produced from the soda ash by calcining (heating) at a high temperature. Suddenly a pure alkali, which enabled the production of nice hard bar soap, became widely available, independent of the availability of extensive hardwood forests. Finally, by 1823 the French chemist Chevreul determined the chemical nature of fats and detailed the chemistry of the process of soap making so that soap could be made by recipe with certainty, rather than by trial and error. This allowed for the large scale, controlled production of reproducible, mild soaps from locally available fats and oils. In other words, these discoveries ultimately led to the existence and successes of today's industry giants. And so, they also led to our ability to make cold-process soap as well as enabling large-scale manufacturing that characterized the industrial age.

MODERN-AGE SOAP MAKING

In the early 1950s, Neil Hosler McElroy, president of Procter & Gamble™, was quoted in Time magazine (October 5, 1953) saying that Tide™ was "the first big change in soap making in 2,000 years." The active surfactant in Tide was produced by the sulfonation of the condensation reaction of benzene with olefins. Tide was introduced the same year as the automatic washing machine cleaner.

Over the next 30 to 40 years, synthetic detergents took over the washing detergent market and then began dominating the bar soap market as detergent bar soaps were introduced. Today, if you can find them, traditional Ivory® (bar) soap and Ivory Snow® laundry soap are the only products that appear on the market claiming the "99 and 44 one-hundredths percent pure" slogan developed when a Procter & Gamble chemist analyzed their soap product. What we usually consider to be soap usually is either a synthetic detergent (syndet) in compressed solid form or a blend of soap with synthetic detergent (a combar). These products infiltrated the market because they lathered well in hard water and did not produce the infamous bathtub ring. Of course, a good marketing campaign suggesting new is both improved and better than old did not hurt either.

THE PRESERVATION OF TRADITIONAL SOAP MAKING

Places still exist where traditional soap-making processes are preserved, protected and valued. In fact, these products are both known for and promoted for their intrinsic value. In the city of Marseille, in the Provence region of France, you can still find Savon de Marseille produced by traditional methods. In fact, in 1688, France passed a law protecting the identity of this soap and specifying the composition and region of manufacture. According to the Savon de Marseille Web site, *www.savondemarseille.com*, this soap still is made using blends of olive and vegetable oils, alkaline ash from sea plants and Mediterranean Sea water. Their process requires two weeks, including 10 days of boiling and heating in antique kettles, followed by pouring "into open pits," cutting and air drying. The fine white powder of sea salt on the surface as well as its natural mildness distinguishes this soap.

A selection of traditional soaps from Savon de Marseille.

THE MYSTIQUE OF AFRICAN BLACK SOAP

African Black Soap is a topic that never fails to generate interest for a wide variety of reasons. Sometimes people simply get word-of-mouth information about its reputation for healing a wide variety of skin problems. Some are interested in ethnic products, either to support ethnic minority businesses or to embrace the use of products designed specifically (and historically) for ethnic minorities. In either case, African Black Soap is a natural product, which has a definite mystique or cachet about it. For these reasons, we will offer a detailed discussion of this unique all-natural product.

Ose Dudu, Dudu-Osen, Anago Soap or *Alata* Soap (Samina) are some of the regional names for this product; and modern-day descendents from Ghana, Togo, Nigeria, Benin and ancient Nubia all claim to be the makers of the original and best soap under any of these names. Even the composition of this product is not universal, since the composition depends on the historic availability of key ingredients in a particular region. Undoubtedly, individual recipes are closely guarded and passed down to the dominantly female family or tribal line since women are the traditional and historic people who gather, harvest and process the key ingredients.

Minor ingredients vary by region. Palm kernel oil, palm oil and coconut oil all are used to a greater or lesser extent, depending on the region, with more coconut oil used in coastal countries, while more shea butter is used in the Savanna regions. There are claims that the color reflects the oils used in the soap, but this is at best only partial truth. The color comes from a combination of orange-looking (carotenoid) pigments in the oils along with the vegetable matter that was used to produce the lye used in the soap. However, the primary ingredient is always shea butter, used at a minimum of 45 percent of the oils.

The uniquely dark (sometimes black) color of the soap comes in part from using vegetable lye produced from burnt leaves. Plantain leaves and skins are the primary source of the lye, though agow bark, palm tree leaves, coco pods, shea tree bark and the shea nut hull residue are among the other materials used. This material is carefully burned to convert the mineral content to the alkaline oxides, which will saponify the oils. Then water is added to the ash, which converts the oxides to the hydroxides, and the lye may or may not be filtered. The dryness of the leaves and other vegetable matter burned, along with the rate at which it is burned, determines the amount of residual carbon in the ash. The amount of filtration, if any, determines the ultimate color of the soap. Unfiltered lye contains more suspended carbon, which produces a darker soap.

AFRICAN BLACK SOAP'S UNIQUE INGREDIENTS

The secret ingredient is *raw or unrefined shea butter*. Shea butter comes from an African tree, *Vitellaria paradoxa*, which generally is not suitable for culture though it is a prevalent wild tree throughout a wide portion of Africa. The shea fruit is roughly plum size and gathered by hand. The traditional process of extracting the fat content is laborious and involves removing the outer pulp of the fruit, shelling the nut using a mortar and pestle or grinding with rocks, roasting the nuts and grinding or pressing the residue to extract the fat. It takes an estimated 20 to 30 hours of labor to produce one kilogram of handcrafted shea butter by traditional methods, though modern equipment can speed up the processing and the fat can be extracted with hexane. Women performing this work are often exploited and, although they work for 30 hours — almost a week's worth of work — they often do not receive even a dollar for their efforts.

Shea butter has one of the highest unsaponifiable content of any oil. Avocado oil has a typical unsap content of up to 6 percent, but shea butter typically has unsaps of 7 to 9 percent or even as high as 13 percent. These unsaps belong primarily to two distinct chemical groups.

The first group is triterpenes, 30 carbon linear and polycyclic hydrocarbons related to squalene (similar to fatty materials in the skin) and the polycyclic sterols. These sterols probably are responsible for the antifungal properties attributed to shea butter. Additionally, much of the triterpene content is in the form of cinnamyl esters. Cinnamic acid absorbs UV rays and so some shea butter formulations are used as mild (up to an SPF of about six) sunblocks.

Closely related to the triterpenes are the carotenoids (vitamin A precursors) and tocopherols (vitamin E). Both classes of compounds are prevalent in the unsaponifiables of shea butter. The other major group in the unsaps include polyphenolic antioxidants, catechins and a family called flavonoids, which are closely related to the antioxidants found in green tea leaves.

Functionally, then, the non-oil content of shea butter is thought to function by both replacing natural skin oils (preserving the natural plasticity of skin) and adding antioxidants, which protect the skin from damage by the elements as well as providing protection from the chemical degradation caused by oxygen. Is it any wonder, then, that the skin ailments treated by shea butter and African Black Soap include: extreme dryness, psoriasis, eczema, dermatitis, skin allergies, fungal infections, blemishes, wrinkles, stretch marks, scars and scrapes? Unfortunately, this panacea for a multitude of skin conditions has one problem — shea butter also is a primary nutrient for the people making the soap. There is a definite conflict between the value of the shea nuts as a source of nutrition and their value as a commercial feedstock. Like many other natural resources, it often is the people who are exploited.

LUXURIOUS NATURAL HANDMADE SOAP: 10 REASONS TO MAKE YOUR OWN

After a while, it all comes down to the question: Why? Why make soap when you can buy it at the grocery store? The answers, or at least our answers, describe the wonderful natural goodness of cold-process soap.

1: Handmade soap retains all the natural glycerin in the soap, unlike most commercial bars. Glycerin is a natural emollient that dramatically boosts lather and provides a milder soap that is gentler to the skin. Glycerin is removed from commercial bars since it is a valuable chemical in its own right — more valuable than the soap.

2: Handmade soap not only uses sustainable resources, it's environmentally friendly. The materials fats and oils you use in cold-process soap are natural ingredients from crops that are either perennial or can be re-grown yearly. Many are plantation raised and organic (the availability of organic feedstocks increases yearly). Many synthetic surfactants are derived partially or completely from petroleum. Our feedstocks of choice are natural oils and fats. Not only is there growing concern for environmentally friendly products, many consumers are now purchasing green products whenever they are given this alternative. In other words, it not only makes good sense as stewards of our natural resources and the environment, it makes good business sense as well.

3: Handmade soap is formulated for you. A balanced combination of coconut, palm, olive, soy and canola (or your favorite) oils produces a superior soap. You don't have to make a large profit at 50 cents a bar using only cheap ingredients in the most economical recipes. Coconut oil gives superior lather; palm oil or vegetable shortening makes for a harder, longer-lasting bar; olive oil, canola oil and lard are especially mild and skin-nourishing components. Superior performance costs more!

4: Each recipe is unique. It bears repeating that the recipes need not change whenever coconut oil increases in price by a nickel. Many people want to make an all-vegetable soap, free of animal products and without animal testing (except on family and friends). When you make the soap, you have total control over the ingredients.

5: Many commercial "soaps" actually are detergent bars. These soap bars are based on synthetic detergents instead of all-natural ingredients. Synthetics can be harsher to your skin than natural soap, especially without the natural glycerin.

6: Handmade soaps can be made with the same costly emollients used in the finest cosmetic lotions and creams. Cocoa butter and shea butter from the African karite tree, our native jojoba oil, beeswax, milk and milk solids, oatmeal and honey — all natural ingredients — are included for their superior mildness and moisturizing properties.

7: You control the choice of colorants and fragrances. Most people who are allergic to soaps and detergents actually are allergic to the colorants and/or the synthetic fragrances. Colors and fragrances can be selected from herbs, natural or high-tech synthetic pigments, essential oils steam-distilled from herbs and high-quality fragrance oils. Selections based on herbal medicine and aromatherapy can result in product(s) that have beneficial properties as well as a pleasing fragrance and a long history of safe and responsible use among humans. Many of the essential oils often used require hundreds of pounds of herbs to produce a single pound of essential oil.

8: Handmade soaps are long lasting. Properly designed cold-process soap will last as long as a commercial soap bar, and longer than many brands.

9: Assured quality. We personally make our soap — handcrafting each bar — watching and assuring the quality of starting materials and finished products. We age our soaps for almost a full month, sometimes longer, before we consider them ready to sell and use. This assures the quality and mildness we have designed into our product.

10: Our name and reputation are part of our products. We are proud of our handmade soap and our reputation for quality is just as important as the vegetable oils we use. We are happy to please our customers. If you should have a problem with our handcrafted soap, we are here; we are not nameless, faceless cogs in a huge corporation. It's a great feeling! Make soap with us and share the feeling of pride and accomplishment.

— Chapter Two —
SAFETY FIRST

The first and most important step, in fact the most critical in any soap-making process, is safety. The major factors that contribute to safe and successful soap making are: an awareness and appreciation of the hazards inherent in the materials and equipment you are using; regular and consistent use of personal safety devices; and, of course, a recipe that will give you a safe, consistent product.

As a practicing chemist and teacher for over 40 years, Bob has gained a feeling that most accidents are caused by one of two things — ignorance or contempt. That is, someone untrained may not appreciate the hazards involved in using a power tool over or near to water. This accounts for the number of people every year who are electrocuted using power saws where there is open groundwater. This accounts for people who accidentally cut through live power lines when they simply want to remove some drywall to do repairs. And ignorance of the hazards can account for the few who are poisoned or burned by unlabeled and misused lye solutions. Contempt, as we use it, actually refers to complaisance. When we are accustomed to dealing with hazardous substances, it is all too easy to allow distractions. We have safely handled something for years without an accident so we start forgetting safety equipment. After all, since we never have an accident, why do we need gloves, goggles and exhaust fans?

PERSONAL PROTECTION

We really need to focus on the hazards that are inherent in the tools of our trade whether it is a hobby or business. Recipes, even the best recipes, will not protect you unless you know and prepare for the normal hazards of production. Simply speaking, you need to protect yourself, use the right pots and stirrers, and protect your family and friends. Personal protection is a necessity.

You should be equipped with gloves, glasses, apron, shoes and knowledge. Gloves protect your hands — thin close-fitting, disposable rubber gloves that do not interfere with your fingers are the best. Latex-free gloves are available if you have allergies. Goggles and glasses protect your eyes from fumes and splashes, especially from lye solutions, which are highly corrosive. A simple apron protects your clothing and body. And shoes, obviously, protect your feet. Of course, knowledge is the hard part.

Watch the accompanying DVD to see a soap-making demonstration using lye.

USING LYE

The largest safety concern focuses on the use of lye. This is a poison if taken internally and it also can cause very serious burns if it comes in contact with your skin or eyes in solid or liquid form. It also can react with aluminum, tin and copper, eating right through these materials. In addition, dissolving solid sodium hydroxide (lye) in water generates a lot of heat — enough to boil water if the amount of water is small or if the water is warm to start.

Bob recently checked the temperatures during the solution process and 125 grams (4 ounces) of lye in 250 grams (8 ounces) of room-temperature water (which combine to give a 33 percent lye solution) brought the temperature to 194 F (90 C). This is uncomfortably close to the boiling point of 212 F (100 C), which generates steam. The vapors (including the steam) given off when sodium hydroxide is added to water are noxious, irritating and burning to your eyes and lungs. So operate with plenty of ventilation, preferably outdoors with the wind at your back or on the back of the stove under a strong hood vent. Always use room-temperature water or even chilled water.

Avoid unsafe temperatures; use a thermometer.

Vinegar can be used to neutralize small lye spills on countertops. However, in case of skin or eye contact, flush the injured part with lots and lots of tepid (room temperature) water either under the faucet or in the shower. For splashes, especially in the eyes — *see a doctor right away.* If you make up your lye solution ahead of time or make extra for later use, label it and keep it away from any other containers where it might be mistaken for something else.

Do not store lye solutions where you store food and beverages. There are terrible stories of people accidentally drinking lye and spending weeks in the hospital recovering from the internal burns. Lye should be stored in a closed container because it will absorb carbon dioxide from the air and slowly convert into sodium carbonate, which will not easily saponify oils. It is a good idea to have the phone number of a poison control center posted near the phone. In the U.S. the number is 800-222-1222.

Always check the label on all the ingredients you use. Sodium and potassium hydroxide virtually look the same, but they are not interchangeable. Sodium hydroxide produces solid soap while potassium hydroxide produces (mostly) liquid soap. Each has different use levels for various oils. It is very easy to mix them up if you have both available.

While you should avoid working near inquisitive children and pets, you should not work alone in the house either. If you spill lye or set your oils on fire (*they are flammable*), it is good to have another pair of hands to help out. If your child or scout troop insists on a soap-making demonstration, consider showing them the melt-and-pour or rebatched soap process.

SAFETY PRECAUTIONS

Other safety items to have around include baking soda and fire extinguishers rated for flammable liquids. However, you do have to be careful not to splash burning oil around the kitchen by overzealous application of a fire extinguisher. A close-fitting lid often is the method of choice to put out an oil fire, as putting the lid in place (carefully) can deny oxygen to the fire and put it out. A damp cloth towel can be used to wipe up fresh soap spills, minimizing risk of contact.

Some safety precautions involve the arrangement of your workspace. Keep electric cords away from sinks. Make sure there are no loose items on the floor, which would be tripping hazards. Arrange your mold(s) so that you minimize distance. Cover surfaces with disposable materials such as butcher's paper so that any spills can be simply folded up and thrown away (if allowed by local ordinance). Properly made, soap will generate virtually no waste. Everything you use should simply become soap. If you have to discard something, check on allowable waste disposal methods and locations.

One final word of wisdom: *Check your insurance coverage*, especially if you scale up your business to selling large quantities or even sell to specialty shops. What is *your* liability? You often can get an umbrella policy for your homeowners insurance that would cover many hazards, including guests slipping, or a customer getting soap in their eyes. If you cannot get coverage under a personal umbrella, check around for reliable insurance companies. You usually can get reliable leads or referrals through the Handcrafted Soapmakers Guild or specialty journals such as the online magazine, Saponifier.

— Chapter Three —
EQUIPMENT YOU NEED TO GET THE JOB DONE

There are many ways to make soap and the essential equipment often depends on which process you use. Heat-resistant silicone ovenware makes great molds that are super-easy to use and clean. Crockpots with removable ceramic inserts make life much simpler for those who venture into hot-process soap. And a stick blender, while not exactly new, deservedly has a prominent place in the arsenal for both cold- and hot-process soap makers.

UTENSILS

Glass, plastic and metal items used for soap making can be safely used for food contact as long as they are thoroughly cleaned after use. Porous items, such as wooden spoons, should not be used again for food and may deteriorate over time due to the action of the lye. Soaking in vinegar after each use may help prolong the life of these items, but eventually they will start to splinter and disintegrate.

The lye solution should be made in a heat-resistant glass container, such as a Pyrex® measuring cup. The cup volume should be large enough to accommodate both the water and the lye with room to spare. A four-cup measuring cup should suffice for a 340g (12-ounce) can of lye plus 600ml to 700ml of water (about 2-½ to 3 cups). Over time, the glass will appear cloudy or scratched. This etching process is a normal result of contact with strong lye solutions. If the etching becomes severe, the glass may be weakened and should be replaced. Some plastics can be used, but keep in mind that the plastic has to survive almost boiling water. Most plastic or glass containers that are labeled microwave safe may be used for the lye solution.

A large pot or pan is needed for the actual soap making. We recommend one that can accommodate twice the volume of the total liquid ingredients. The construction preferably should be stainless steel, though a ceramic-lined pot will work. Aluminum, copper and tin are not suitable. Lye solutions will react with aluminum, sometimes violently, eating away the container and forming hydrogen gas as a byproduct. Hydrogen is a highly flammable, explosive gas. Remember the *Hindenberg*, the German dirigible filled with hydrogen that caught fire, burned and crashed in New Jersey just prior to the start of World War II?

Iron (like cast iron) is not always suitable either, mainly due to rust formation that will turn your soap reddish brown. However, cast iron generally is used for reenactment soap making demonstrations, so it definitely will survive and the soap will be usable. And although we question the overall suitability, cast iron was used in soap making for hundreds of years without problem. We also have seen warnings to avoid Teflon™ and other nonstick-coated pots as well, probably due to the ease of marring the surface and exposing the base metal of the pot.

Lye and a measuring cup large enough to accomadate the water/lye solution.

Chapter Three: Equipment You Need to Get the Job Done

Digital models offer precise temperature controls,
but nothing beats a good thermometer to assure you of the temperature of the contents.

CROCKPOTS AND COMPANION TOOLS

If you use a crockpot, select the deepest crock you can find. The capacity is not nearly as important as the depth; the disadvantage being the ability of hot reacting soap to splash out of the pot. Virtually all crockpots now have a removable insert, but don't resurrect that old pot from your basement. Buy one with a removable crock — it is worth the investment. Crockpots today have two different types of controls, both suitable. There is absolutely no problem with a pot having controls that read, "keep warm, low, high." In fact, you probably will use the warm and low controls more than the high.

Use stainless steel or dishwasher-safe plastic stirring spoons, paddles, dippers and spatulas. (Common kitchen plastic or rubber spatulas are quite useful in getting that last bit of soap out of your pot.) We previously used a long plastic paddle with holes in the paddle that we found in a local home-brewing supply store. Now that we have been converted, we use a stick blender.

Hand blenders, also known as stick blenders (not hand mixers) should be used with care. (This type of blender was designed to mix drinks in a glass.) Immerse prior to turn-

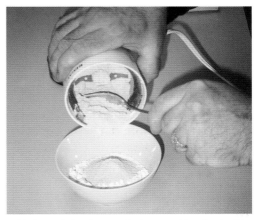

Herbs and abrasives are finely ground in a food mill before being added to soap.

ing on and start with a low setting. Be sure it has no immersible parts made of aluminum.

Stick blenders have two drawbacks. One is the tendency of piping-hot lye-heavy soap solution splashing up the sides of the pot when mixing. It takes careful practice to get used to handling a stick blender, while avoiding splashing the liquid soap all over you and the surrounding counter. Believe us — the time saved makes it well worth the effort and practice! However, when you use a stick blender, do not allow your children in the area or allow them to do the stirring. Use a splash guard of some sort — a lid covering most of the opening will do. Or use a pot with very high walls.

It takes careful practice to get used to handling a stick blender.

The second drawback is that the stick blender can take you to a thick trace in 10 to 20 minutes, depending on the temperatures and formulations you use. The speed may be an advantage, but you have to be ready to move from the pot to the mold in very short order. As the mixture gets thick, it becomes very difficult to stir in the color and fragrance. You have to add these at thin trace when the unreacted lye concentration is still high. Herbs will not be stable under these conditions and will brown. Vitamin E and rosemary oil extract (ROE) may not suffice to preserve herbal color and fragrance under these conditions. Our advice: Start small and prove out your recipe and your approach. It may not be possible to use the same reaction conditions for every type of soap you make.

Yes, electric beaters or mixers can be used, but hand-held units are difficult to use without splashing; a better approach is the stand-type mixer with a splash guard. Blenders also can be used if you are sure the blades are stainless steel. Using a blender does limit your batch size. And you need to be sure the agitation doesn't knock the top off the blender, spraying lye and oil everywhere.

If you want to make large batches, 9kg to 15kg (20 to 30 pounds) at a time, visit your hardware store and get a paint mixer attachment for your drill. They also probably have some large clamps to hold it in place while it is running — great if you are working in five gallon or larger sizes. The lower price also beats the hundreds of dollars for a commercial variable-speed motor and mixer shaft. Be sure it is *all steel*, not aluminum.

A stainless steel whisk may prove useful if you intend to add powdered ingredients during saponification. Herbs, pumice, clay and the like are readily dispersed using a whisk. For large batches, you may want to remove a portion of the soap stock, disperse the herbs in the stock and then add this mixture back to the bulk of the soap. Any small food mill used for grinding coffee can be used to grind dried herbs into powder. You may wish to put this powdered material through a sieve to be sure the grind is fine enough for use.

Buy a stainless steel thermometer with either a dial-type or immersion-type reading and a range of 86 F to 230 F (30 C to 110 C). Ninety degrees Fahrenheit (32 C) probably is the practical lower temperature limit for cold-process soap and you only need to reach temperatures as high as 230 F (110 C) if you are rebatching.

MOLDS

You may use a wide variety of objects as molds. Ordinarily, the mold will be made of plastic or lined with plastic wrap (or butcher's or waxed paper).

Plastic wrap makes it very simple to release the soap and you can scale it up or down as you please. Plastic candy or candle molds will work nicely. One of the simplest molds is a quart-size waxed milk carton, thoroughly washed and dried. PVC pipe should be carefully sealed with plastic wrap, a flat end cap or a (removable) wax plug. Even small lengths of pipe can be distorted with heat and pressure

PVC pipe, usually 8cm (3") in diameter, has been used successfully as a mold. Use either the round or downspout-shaped types.

If you are handy with wood and tools, you can make a hinged box for a mold that easily comes apart. Line it with plastic wrap for easy release of soap.

to form an oval mold. The mold should either be somewhat flexible or disposable.

Particularly useful molds for round and rectangular bars are those made for resin casting and found in many hobby shops. And of course, soap-making supply companies offer specialized molds in many fanciful shapes, including those which produce a highly embossed bar.

Not long ago, most new soap makers used plastic drawer organizers as their first mold. This produces a nice loaf of soap that can be easily cut into smaller bars. Now, however, *the choice is simpler and better — silicone.*

Kitchen stores and department stores alike carry a large line of silicone cookware. Square cake pans make excellent molds, as do the large variety of muffin pans. You also can use the silicone cupcake liners for smaller or designer bars. But we offer some words of caution. Leaving soap in a mold for a week or more tends to degrade the surface. This may not have a lasting impact on the mold, but

These individual molds are available in sizes from 74ml to 118ml (2.5 to 4 ounces) and are easy to fill, handle and clean.

it is enough to be of concern. On the other hand, soap is always ready to unmold in two days and we have not seen any problems over this period of time. Another potential concern with silicone molds is their flexibility. If you plan to move them once filled, you need to keep them on a pan (stainless steel is best) so that you do not cause the mold to flex and spill the contents.

Use a rigid base when moving your soap in flexible molds to avoid spilling.

The silicone mold can be easily peeled away from the hardened soap.

Chapter Three: Equipment You Need to Get the Job Done

You can bake a cake with these pans so they are designed to move a bit, but cake batter is cold and will not cause burns if spilled on your skin. The lye in the soap mixture, however, is still very much a danger and must be handled with caution. One solution to this problem came from a trip to a kitchenware store where we found KitchenAid® silicone muffin molds set into a rigid metal framework — all the advantages of silicone with the stability of metal.

Although these are embossing molds for single bars, large embossed molds for nine to 12 bars are readily available.

Chapter Three: Equipment You Need to Get the Job Done

STORAGE

You'll need a place to store your soap while it ages or cures. When we were first learning to make soap at home, we used what we thought were stainless steel wire racks to store our soap during curing, since they would allow air circulation on all sides of the bars. Apparently these racks were chromed steel and probably a little worn. They left brownish wire marks on the bottom of the soap, which penetrated well into the bar. At the time, we viewed this as functionally okay, but aesthetically displeasing. In retrospect, we probably were observing examples of initial oxidation catalyzed by the iron in the rack. A similar process occasionally will form orange spots — "Dreaded Orange Spots" (DOS) — on the surface of the soap during storage; this is thought to be the first stages of the soap turning rancid. Although orange spots can be avoided through use of an antioxidant such as rosemary oil extract (ROE), it is better to avoid conditions that promote oxidation.

You'll also need a storage container for your finished soap. There are some quite inexpensive plastic "sweater boxes" available at specialty kitchen stores and in the kitchen department of discount stores. These boxes

Extreme example of "Dreaded Orange Spots" on soap from air oxidation. This can occur with highly superfatted soap or with soap stored in hot moist conditions.

have lids so the essential oils won't evaporate over time and the plastic is non-reactive to or with your soap. They do, however, retain moisture. Care must be taken to cure the soap well prior to storing it in this sort of box lest the moisture migrate to the surface and promote rancidity. A good old-fashioned shoe box also will serve well. Separate the layers of soap with clean unprinted paper.

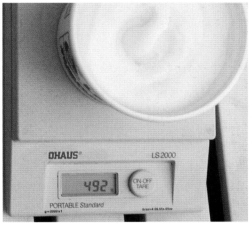

One of many suitable types of digital scales. This scale has a tare function and is weighing a container of lard.

MEASURING TOOLS

You'll need to measure and judge your proportions by weight, not volume. Measuring cups are not accurate enough. The best type of balance or scale to start with is an electronic balance that measures in grams or tenths of grams with a capacity of 500 to 5,000 grams. One with the ability to tare (automatically subtract the weight of your container) would be ideal. OHAUS® makes a scale readable to one gram, priced well under $100. Food balances also are available for $40 to $80 with a capacity of 4.5kg to 9kg (10 to 20 pounds), reading to about 1.8g (¹⁄₁₆ ounce). Remember, *these scales are for your ingredients — not the finished bars.* If you intend to sell the soap bars by weight, you are required to use an *inspected and certified scale.* This may vary somewhat from state to state and country to country, but generally speaking, the requirement is universal.

— Chapter Four —

BASIC INGREDIENTS

Soap comes from a type of compound called triglycerides —
fats and oils. Saponification, the chemical reaction that produces
soap and glycerin, converts virtually any animal fat or vegetable
oil into soap. Selection is key to the properties you desire:
coconut and palm kernel oils contribute to lather; common
vegetable oils and fats contribute to mildness; and many oils have
additional components, which contribute emolliency (essentially
add a soft skin feel).

The following chapter describes the various alternatives you can use to start making your soap. In some cases we point out the potential problems or benefits from using specific starting materials. This chapter will help you shop wisely for your materials and the recipes in later chapters will show you how to use them to produce wonderful handmade soap.

You also have the choice of using many supplemental ingredients that will enhance the overall quality of the soap and the soap-making experience. Make your personal statement by the ingredients you select.

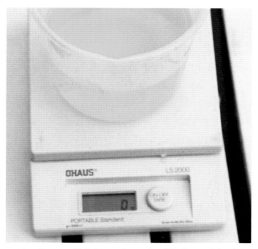
A mixture of jojoba and canola oil being weighed.

FATS, OILS, BUTTERS, HERBS, ETC.

In general, lard and vegetable oils purchased at the grocery store should be suitable for soap making, whereas grass-fed bison fat is a specialty fat. It has a natural high vitamin A (antioxidant) content because it is grass fed and should be distinguished from bison that are "finished" by grain feeding. The grain-finished bison fat will be much whiter and it has little natural antioxidant content. The people who raise and sell 100-percent grass-fed bison and bison fat (see page 90) use every part of the animal — nothing is wasted. The spirit of the Plains is preserved by this natural, green tradition.

Be advised that olive oil comes in several varieties and grades. Olive pomace oil frequently is used for soap since it is about 10 to 15 percent less costly than virgin olive oils. Solvent extraction of the olive pits and other residue of previous pressing frequently manufacture pomace oil. However, other pomace oils also are available and can be easily confused. If you use pomace oil, read the fine print and be sure the product is 100 percent olive derived. Inferior grades of pomace may have unacceptably high peroxide value, which can lead to rancidity in the finished soap unless a stabilizing antioxidant, vitamin E or ROE, is added. Although any grade probably can be used, olive oil tends to have a distinctive odor, which in some grades is quite pronounced. The color and odor of the oils used usually will be present to a slight degree in the finished soap. If you are going to delicately scent your soap, use one of the lighter, less odorous grades of oil.

The highest quality of soap usually contains olive oil.

Specialty and Asian grocery stores often carry coconut oil in 454g to 1,360g (1- to 3-pound) quantities. You might also try your local bakery or movie house (if they pop their own popcorn). If you explain your purpose, they may sell you what they purchase. You are looking for what is known as white coconut oil (avoid butter-flavored and colored). Some restaurant supply companies stock it. Many essential-oil dealers also handle coconut, jojoba and soybean oils, and some may carry palm oil as well. Most companies that specifically sell soap-making supplies will offer all the common oils and many specialty oils as well. Columbus Foods, located near Chicago, Illinois, offers a special section of vegetable oils for soap making.

A 324g (12-ounce) plastic can of lye being poured into deionized water to make a lye solution.

LYE

Alas, lye can no longer be found on the grocery store shelf. Safety concerns and liability caused Red Devil™ Lye to exit the consumer market. There are a number of chemical suppliers, such as The Boyer Corporation, that will sell to soap makers and you also can purchase various quantities from any of the suppliers of soap ingredients. We listed several of our favorites in the Resources section on page 149. It is still possible to find lye in a few hardware stores, but usually by special order.

Avoid drain openers that contain both lye and aluminum metal. These often come in a similar can and the aluminum metal liberates hydrogen gas when dissolved in water. (The reason for this is that most drain plugs are caused by a combination of oil or fat and hair. The lye supplies heat to melt the fat and, in combination with hydrogen and aluminum, starts a chemical reaction that breaks down hair protein making it easier to flush down the drain.)

Many people ask why we use lye to make soap — lye is so harsh and dangerous. Lye is the most convenient and cheapest alkali readily available. It is important to remember that lye is an intermediate used to make soap; it is not an ingredient in your finished soap unless you have added extra, which normally is not at all desirable. That is, you plan to have all the lye consumed by the fats and oils, leaving none behind as an ingredient. Remember this if you plan to label your soap at some point.

Potassium hydroxide (caustic potash) is another soap ingredient found only from soap ingredient suppliers and chemical supply houses. It usually is found as 3mm (⅛") pellets (about the size of split peas) that are 85 percent potassium hydroxide and 15 percent water. It is important to take this water into consideration when you formulate recipes. Potassium hydroxide ordinarily is reserved for the formation of soft and liquid soaps, since the potassium soaps are significantly more water-soluble than the sodium soaps. Soft soaps ordinarily result when potassium hydroxide is used together with a recipe rich in liquid oils, especially if the recipe is superfatted to at least 5 percent.

Sodium or potassium carbonate (soda ash and potash respectively) could be used in place of lye since the process of saponification can, under certain conditions, produce free fatty acids, which are almost instantly neutralized to their salts. The carbonates are harder to locate than lye and they liberate carbon dioxide when they react with acids, which should lead to the generation of foam. They also are much less reactive than lye and usually require strong heating to complete their reactions.

Baking soda generally is considered to be unsuitable for saponification, being substantially less reactive. Several citations in most soap-making literature indicate that baking soda will not saponify fats and oils. It is, however, sometimes used in rendering to remove acidic contaminants from tallow without saponifying any of the fat.

WATER

Don't forget about water. Use distilled water whenever possible, though you might want to try collecting and using rainwater, which is, in theory, nature's own version of distilled water. Typically, tap water is too hard and contains too much magnesium and calcium ion, which produces insoluble fatty acid salts (soap scum). Bottled spring water is not necessarily any softer than tap water. A workable alternative is soft water from a water softener or reverse osmosis purifier. The soft water should be low in iron as well as magnesium and calcium, since iron salts at high pH will turn brown due to formation of iron hydroxides, a gelatinous precipitate.

Rainwater can be collected as nature's own version of distilled water.

Formation of these iron hydroxides also will consume part of your lye solution. There are several hand-held demineralizing (water softening) units now on the market with replaceable cartridges. These make fully acceptable substitutes for bottled water.

Unless you make cosmetic or medical claims for your soap, you are not required by the Food and Drug Administration (FDA) to list the ingredients on the label. Examples of cosmetic claims are skin softening or moisturizing; examples of medical claims are anti-acne or anti-dandruff.

— Chapter Five —
ADDITIVES TO CUSTOMIZE SOAP

Soaps ordinarily are designed to contain a wide variety of additives, color and fragrance being the most common. Essential oils, pressed, extracted or distilled from various plants, are most often used since they tend to be relatively stable during the highly alkaline soap-making process. Essential oils from herbs have various therapeutic benefits and dried herbs can produce color and fragrance. Fragrance oils, although synthetic, are blended to emulate natural fragrances.

Soap colors produced using Food & Drug approved dyes. Top row, left to right: yellow No. 5, yellow No. 6, yellow No. 10, green No. 3, green No. 5. Bottom row: blue No. 1, red No. 28, red No. 30 Lake, red No. 33, red No. 33 Lake.

COLORANTS

We strongly recommend that you request a Material Safety Data Sheet (MSDS) from any reputable supplier of chemicals and read it carefully before you put a chemical in contact with the skin for any purpose. Cosmetic grade pigments are readily available, assuring that there are no harmful levels of heavy metals or other contaminants that could prove injurious to the user. Both pigments and Food, Drug and Cosmetic (FD&C) dyes are quite effective. Fifteen milliliters (one tablespoon) of pigment is often sufficient to color 3.6kg to 4.5kg (8 to 10 pounds) of soap.

Colorants often are unfairly categorized as either natural or unnatural. The natural includes most pigments as well as the true natural products, herbs and herbal extracts. Unnatural colorants include various types of synthetic dyes. In simpler times, pigments were mined (they still are in limited production in Provence, France). However, it virtually is impossible to find these pigments in the U.S. — most are synthetic — in that they are produced by the controlled chemical oxidation of various iron and other transition metals. Chemically, the pigments are identical to the mined product but are inaccessible in the United States. We do not know what restrictions apply to Canadian soap makers.

Various experts argue about the ability of either dye or pigment to produce vivid or intense colors. Rather than argue the case, we simply present the results of a series of experiments using a wide variety of both materials. Examine the photographic evidence and decide for yourself.

It is relatively simple to use readily available *vegetable dyes* to tint and color soap; however, most allergic reactions are caused by either colorants (dyes) or fragrances — natural or synthetic. Some FD&C dyes can be used to color soap but they all are not stable under the very highly alkaline conditions of soap making (many rapidly fade when exposed to sunlight). Drug and Cosmetic (D&C) dyes are approved for use in various types of drugs and cosmetics. FD&C dyes may also be used in foods. Those useful or approved for soap have been approved for use in various applications, often (but not always) for skin contact only.

Compare the actual dye powders to the colors they produce in soap.

VEGETABLE MATERIALS AS COLORANTS

Many **vegetable materials** are readily available for use as colorants.

- **Annatto, turmeric and paprika** produce shades of yellow to orange.

- **Carotene**, naturally present in red palm oil and often available in gel caps in the pharmacy, produces an orange color.

- **Red sandalwood** produces a purple (at a typical use level of roughly 15ml [1 tablespoon] per 4.5kg [10 pounds] of oil).

- **Cocoa** is sometimes used for brown, though it also is possible to get a nice medium brown by adding herbs without an antioxidant.

- **Chlorophyll**, often found in pharmacies in the form of gel caps, produces a reasonable green.

- **Green herbs**, when stabilized with vitamin E, can also be used to make green herbal bars.

- We recently discovered that **green kelp**, purchased from a food co-op, makes a very satisfactory medium green and does not require the addition of vitamin E stabilizer.

- **Carmine or cochineal** (derived from the shell of a beetle) is an approved source of many pinks to reds, though it is not especially fat-soluble, so aqueous extracts should be prepared and used.

- **Powdered alkanet root** gives a blue to bluish-purple color, and often is used by steeping the powder in oil, extracting the color into the oil.

- **Powdered oatmeal** with or without honey will impart a warm, light brown color (and produce an aroma like cookies).

As with so many other special ingredients, purchase these colorants from someone who deals extensively with soap ingredients and can tell you which dyes are stable. Seven grams (1 tablespoon) of a suitable dye can color 24kg (50 pounds) or more of soap, depending on the desired color intensity. Many suppliers offer *"color tabs" or "nuggets,"* which are dyes diluted with soap. Usage rates vary depending on the supplier, but a single tab or nugget often will color from 900g to 5kg (2 to 6 pounds) of soap.

You also should note that FD&C blue No. 1 will probably produce a pink or mauve color and FD&C green No. 3 will come out more purple or deep blue than green. This is due to the alkaline pH of soap. These two dyes really will produce a blue and a green color, respectively, when used at pH below seven. This is fairly complex chemistry involving very complex molecules, which change structure back and forth between two possibilities as they gain or lose a proton, just as phenolphthalein changes from colorless to pink as the pH becomes alkaline. Take this into

consideration when choosing your colorant.

Some people use *aniline dyes* like those used in candle making to color their soap. These dyes are much more stable than the food colors (FD&C) and are identical or closely related to the chemicals used to dye hair. In the past five to seven years, there have been concerns expressed over the toxicology of hair dyes. Although no link was demonstrated between hair dyes and various forms of cancer, we believe that discretion is the better part of valor and don't recommend the use of aniline dyes.

Pigmenting soap to produce colors is commonplace. *Titanium dioxide* has long been used to produce opaque, bright whites, but pigments generate many beautiful pastels and vivid colors. Pigment can be either natural or synthetic. *Iron-oxide pigments* are extensively mined in Roussillon, Provence, France, and cover a huge range of colors from yellows to reds to browns. Indian red, Turkey red, and Venetian red (covering the range from light to dark) are just a few examples of the range possible in a single color from

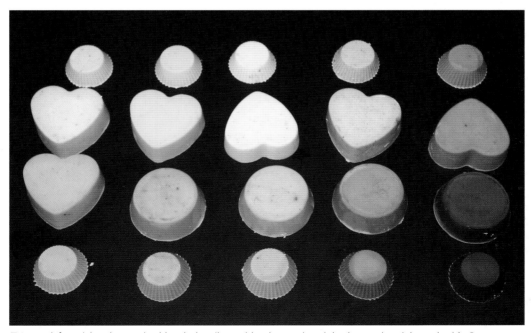

Top row, left to right: ultramarine blue dark, yellow oxide, ultramarine pink, ultramarine violet, red oxide. Bottom row: hydrated chrome oxide, chromium oxide green, ultramarine blue medium, brown oxide, black oxide

Compare the color of the powdered pigment to the color in a finished soap sample.

the iron oxides. The synthetic iron-oxide pigments are just industrial versions of these same naturally occurring materials, prepared from ferrous sulfate, perhaps with a tighter control of particle size. These pigments virtually are water-insoluble, stable to alkali and colorfast in sunlight.

Cold-process soap containing pumice. This soap was made in a quart milk carton but you can slice it into thinner bars.

Pigments also can be functional. *Green and red clays* help to soften skin and can be selected to help "dry" oily skin. *Pumice*, mentioned elsewhere as a mild abrasive, gives a very attractive light gray appearance to the soap. In a broader sense, coffee grounds will give color and act as an exfolient. Coffee soap often is cited as the ideal kitchen soap to deodorize hands that have come in contact with garlic, fish and other penetrating food odors.

Whatever color source you choose, you can achieve interesting and often striking visual effects with the same techniques discussed in Chapter 7 in the section on rebatched soaps. Examples of two- and three-layer soaps and variegated embedded soaps are shown in both Chapters 7 and 8.

ESSENTIAL OILS

There is quite a bit of debate about whether essential oils maintain their healthful properties when used in soap making. Heat during saponification, contact with strong alkali and short contact time during washing all are cited as reasons to doubt the benefit of using essential oils. Direct evidence typically is lacking, though apocryphal accounts abound. Finally, a majority of aromatherapy practitioners agree that essential oils in soap do have at least some, if not all, of their healthful properties if the soap is produced under conditions where the aroma retains the character of the original oil. Even with brief skin contact, it certainly is better to apply a therapeutic essential oil than not. And in any event, inhalation of the fragrance, not the soap, is the easiest mechanism to introduce essential oils into the body by exchange in the nasal mucous membrane. We personally believe in the use of essential oils because we have seen many lingering skin conditions helped by using a soap containing the appropriate essential oils.

An electric food mill, shown here with a mixture of chamomile and ground oatmeal, is very useful for powdering and mixing herbs and coarse pigments before adding them to soap.

Many easy-to-grow herbs such as Echinacea can be added to your soap after they are dried and ground to a powder, or use them to make tea.

ABRASIVES

Abrasives also are fairly common in hand soaps, since they help scour or loosen dirt from nooks and crannies (e.g. under fingernails). Pumice, a porous volcanic rock, can be used as well as a variety of organic materials such as finely ground oatmeal, cornmeal, and nut meal and hulls. Abrasiveness increases roughly in this order: oatmeal, cornmeal, nut meal, nut hulls, pumice. Mild abrasives also function to exfoliate the skin (help slough off old dry skin cells, exposing the softer underlayer). In practical terms for home soap making, 227g to 454g (1 to 2 cups) of abrasive are sufficient in a 4.5kg (10-pound) batch of soap.

EMOLLIENTS

If excess oil (or fatty acid) is added to the soap (more than can react with the lye provided), the soap is termed *superfatted*. In actuality, unreacted fat or oil is unlikely to remain completely unchanged during soap making since there is an excess of water and glycerin available with which to react. The excess oil most likely transforms into a complex mixture of semi-reacted materials such as fatty acids and glycerides. These compounds are well-known *emollients* — skin softeners and moisturizers that actually can be absorbed into the outer layers of the skin and, fortunately, don't leave an oily residue on the skin.

Wide ranges of materials are used commercially today in soap and detergent bars. The simplest are either excess oil or excess fatty acids. Mineral oil, lanolin and fatty alcohols often have been used, but today are of questionable value due to the possibility of clogging skin pores and potentially promoting acne.

SUPERFATTING

For the home soap maker, *superfatting* usually is accomplished by either reducing the calculated lye requirement by a fixed amount (a "lye discount") or by adding extra oil, usually at trace or during a rebatching step. Often, more expensive oils and vegetable butters are added this way so that saponification is kept to a minimum. Levels of superfatting normally range from 1 percent to 15 percent, but levels above 7 percent usually require the addition of an antioxidant to help stabilize and preserve the soap from spoiling. A more desirable range for superfatting is an excess of 3 percent to 5 percent, which ordinarily does not require antioxidants unless the soap is made and stored in a warm moist climate (Hawaii, Florida, etc.).

Other emollients are naturally occurring components of vegetable oils (especially olive oil), which are chemically unrelated to the oils themselves. Emollients are chemically unrelated to oils. These unsaponifiable materials have a variety of chemical forms and are present in quantities from hardly measurable up to 11 percent of the total oil. Although any oil can be used to superfat soap, more expensive, skin-beneficial oils should be added at trace or during rebatching to preserve the properties of the oil, which are often lost by saponification. The principal role of these natural emollients in soap and cosmetics, however, is as an occlusive agent — a fatty material deposited on the skin to retard moisture loss and keep the skin from drying out.

PROTEIN

Protein often is added for skin and hair softening. There are several natural sources of protein available to the home soap maker, the simplest being milk. Cleopatra reportedly bathed in milk (goat, mare or ass, depending on the story you hear) for her fabled complexion. Today, goat milk usually is available in most parts of the country and powdered goat milk is available at many health food and grocery stores. It's also possible to dissolve silk, a natural protein material, in lye and use this in your soap making. *Oatmeal*, previously mentioned as a mild abrasive, also imparts a soft smooth character to the skin.

HUMECTANTS AND OTHER ADDITIVES

Other additives, which also are skin moisturizers, include *humectants* such as honey, propylene glycol or glycerin; *lubricants* such as bentonite and other clays used in shaving soaps to provide a thin layer of small platelets to protect the skin as the blade glides across the surface; *antioxidants and stabilizers* such as vitamins A, C and E; and herbal extracts, especially rosemary oil extract (ROE). Certain other raw materials, such as jojoba oil, have both fatty acid and fatty alcohol content, providing high levels of soap together with emollient action from the fatty alcohol. (Jojoba oil has the added benefit of rarely spoiling.)

GLYCERIN

Mass-produced soap generally has the *natural glycerin* removed and so it lacks the natural moisturizer that cold-processed soap retains. Glycerin also tends to boost foaming and so it is sometimes added back to a complexion bar to overcome the lather-suppressing effect of adding the extra fat. Again, in cold-process soap that is superfatted, retained glycerin is the reason we can produce a mild soap with good or superior foaming properties. It even is possible, and often desirable, to add extra glycerin to formulations for shaving soap that benefit from longer-lasting stable foam.

Many commercial soap bars are either partially or totally composed of synthetic detergents. Those without soap generally are called syndets for synthetic detergent. Dove, a leading complexion bar, is reported to be roughly 26 percent stearic acid and 55 percent synthetic detergent (Igepon A). Zest is reportedly a combar — a combination of synthetic detergent and soap —and in this case, a blend of two synthetic detergents (glycerol ether sulfonate and fatty alcohol sulfate) and soap.

— Chapter Six —

CREATING FRAGRANCE – MANY OPTIONS, ALL GOOD

Fragrance creation is like writing an opera. Each fragrance component has a characteristic fragrance note and, when notes are combined and balanced, the result is a full, round fragrance. Many soap makers will let a supplier write the fragrance score while others will make a personal statement by composing the fragrance themselves. In both cases, the fragrance components usually are selected from essential oils, fragrance oils and blends, and herbs (or infusions).

FRAGRANCE FROM ESSENTIAL OILS

Essential oils usually are isolated from the flowers, leaves or roots of a plant by steam distillation. The appropriate part of the herb is placed in or above water in a boiler and this floral mix is boiled, often under reduced pressure. The steam is collected and condensed and the insoluble essential oils rise to the top and are removed. The fragrant water condensate left behind is termed floral water, such as rose water or lavender water. Essential oils are highly concentrated and usually are not suitable to use directly on the skin because of their concentrated nature. The yield of essential oil varies with the plant, but often only a few pounds of oil are obtained from hundreds of pounds of plant. They usually are priced accordingly, but frequently only 15ml or 30ml (1 or 2 teaspoons) are needed to scent 1kg (2.2 pounds) of soap.

The true benefit of essential oils is their historical medicinal use in aromatherapy, which proposes that herbal fragrance can stimulate the brain to affect mental states and physical well-being. There is quite a bit of literature available dealing with the use of specific essential oils to calm, reduce depression or stress, or even stimulate the immune system. Some essential oils, such as lavender oil diluted in carrier (vegetable) oil, also are quite good for the skin and widely used in massage therapy. Although there has been some debate as to the level of benefit derived from using essential oils in soap, the consensus seems to be that if the scent remains true, there should be at least some benefit, in addition to providing a totally natural fragrance. And, since not all fragrance is washed away with the lather, there should be some residual benefit to the skin.

Of course, caution is needed in selecting essential oils for soap, as not all are recommended for skin contact. See the list on pages 121 to 133 for the benefits and effects of different essential oils, including warnings against the use of some commonly available essential oils.

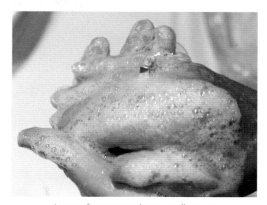

A great fragrance takes a quality soap to an even higher level.

FRAGRANCE FROM FRAGRANCE OILS

You can readily find oils in various hobby and craft stores labeled as fragrance oils. These will not always give satisfactory results unless they are intended for use in soap making. Fragrance oils designed specifically for soap making are available by mail order from a number of suppliers (see Resources on page 149). Vendors should be able to tell you if there will be any adverse effect to your soap-making process, such as causing cold-process soap to seize (see Glossary on page 143). The highest quality fragrance oils often are a blend of natural and synthetic components and may contain as many as 30 separate components. Originally, expert perfumers compounded fragrance oils, relying on their trained noses and experience with fragrance components. Today, using complex modern instrumentation to separate and identify volatile fragrance components, and then blending known components, many fragrance profiles are duplicated.

Fragrance oils, especially for those scents not available (economically) from essential oils, represent another series of perennial favorites. Vanilla, rose, jasmine, lilac, gardenia, almond, apple, chocolate, musk, cucumber and raspberry are always in demand and always attract crowds. The only factor that usually inhibits creativity in blending fragrances is the cost of the essential or fragrance oils. However, with the ability to use cotton swabs to preview your fragrance blends, you can be creative without being wasteful. It's also helpful that many suppliers offer a limited number of small, free or low-cost samples for you to evaluate. Of course — the more expensive the oil — the smaller the sample, but it does provide an opportunity to confirm your hope that you can blend your own winning fragrance.

It is not correct to broadly state that no therapeutic benefit can be obtained from fragrance oil. And as the content of these oils are trade secrets, it also is impossible to say that there are any benefits in using them. The big advantage is that fragrance oils offer a wide range of affordable fragrances, especially those that are not available as essential oils or those that are available but prohibitively expensive. Perfumers tend to use natural and synthetic fragrances together, looking for a final wondrous effect, unconcerned with trying to label their product "natural." And there certainly is nothing wrong with that.

FRAGRANCE FROM EXTRACTS

It's also possible to use extracts such as vanilla, lemon or almond as fragrance. There is nothing wrong with trying, but these extracts are not overly strong smelling. If you need to add a lot to get the desired fragrance level, consider using an essential oil. Often more concentrated extracts designed for professional bakers and food formulators are available. You may be able to purchase the extracts from a local bakery if you explain what you are doing. If you are unable to get the extract locally (they are not sold at the grocery store) you will need to contact the extract maker directly. You also need to consider that most extracts contain at least some alcohol. Too much alcohol can lead to instability in the soap mixture, leading to either oil and water separation or seizing — start on a small scale and be cautious. We've had repeated success using concentrated lemon extracts (together with powdered lemon peel and lemongrass) but have been unable to generate a lasting vanilla aroma using its extract.

Fragrances, that are fragrant oils, come from a variety of sources including plants and animals.

- Citrus oils expressed from the peels of lemon, lime, orange and grapefruit oils.
- Flowers and blossoms from rose petals to cloves and oils obtained from citrus blossoms.
- Leaves and related herbaceous materials. (Typically there is more leaf and stem material than flowers, so oils produced from flowers, leaves and stems tend to be more abundant and less expensive than oil isolated only from flowers.)
- Cinnamon and cassia bark and sassafras root bark.
- Roots and rhizomes of iris, vetiver and ginger.
- Seeds of coriander, caraway, cocoa, anise and many other seeds.
- Lichens such as oak and tree moss.
- Various woods such as sandalwood, rosewood, cedar and juniper.
- Frankincense, myrrh, amber, Peru balsam and gum benzoin, among others. (Resins have been used in perfumery since ancient times.)
- Musk covers a wide range of sources, including musk deer, civet and beaver.
- Ambergris from expelled secretions (okay, it's vomit) from the sperm whale. (Long-prized as a base for perfumes.)

Chapter Six: Creating Fragrance - Many Options, All Good

FRAGRANCE FROM HERBS

In general, herbs should be dried and ground for use in soap, though occasionally herbal teas are used to replace some or all of the water for the lye solution. If you want to avoid darkening of the herbs, incorporate an antioxidant such as vitamin E into your soap. Be aware that vitamin E can be purchased as pure oil as well as in a vegetable-oil carrier such as sesame oil. Vitamin E from "natural" sources such as wheat germ oil also can be used. Vitamin C, another readily available antioxidant, is itself an acid and additional lye should be used to neutralize the acid groups if this is used. Some herbs contain natural antioxidants and do not require additional ingredients. Lavender is the most commonly used herb in soap making, but rosemary, sage, chamomile, hops, lemongrass and many other beneficial herbs are used to enhance the visual and aromatic appeal and skin-soothing properties of soap.

Jojoba or olive oil is added to completely cover the flower blossoms.

The oil and blossom container is covered to keep it free from insects and allowed to sit in the sun.

FRAGRANCE FROM INFUSED OILS

If you have a fragrant garden, it is also possible to make your own infused oils. Here, flowers are covered with oil and either gently heated for an hour or two in the top of a double boiler or left to warm in the sun for 24 to 48 hours. The soaked flowers can then be removed and new flowers added to intensify the fragrance transferred to the oil. Infused oils can be used either as a base oil or added at trace or during rebatch to fragrantly superfat the soap.

The infused oil is filtered and can be stored or used again with more blossoms to increase the intensity of the scent.

The fragrance of natural hyacinth can be captured by infusion.

Not all beautiful natural scents are available as essential oils. A lilac scent can be prepared by infusion or enfleurage, but for a pronounced scent in your soap, you will have to use fragrance oil.

MAKING THE FRAGRANCE DECISION

When it comes to selecting a fragrance for your soap, there are three distinctly different approaches.

1. You can select a single essential or fragrance oil because you like the scent or want the specific healing properties of the essential oil.

2. You can blend two or three essential oils into your soap, based on the reported aromatherapy properties of the oils. (Blends with beneficial effects greater than individual oils are called synergies.) You can choose oils that are uplifting or healing, have a physical effect or an emotional or psychic one. It is generally counterproductive to blend oils with opposing effects, such as calming and invigorating, but you might use lavender essential oil, which is relaxing, with rosemary essential oil, which is energizing, because lavender also can be stimulating since it reduces stress and anxiety.

Once you have selected a number of potential oils to use for scent, you need to blend them harmoniously — the right amount of each oil. A good way to blend oils based on their fragrance, rather than thera-peutic characteristics, is described below. Remember, you have already selected the oils for their therapeutic benefit, now you want to fine-tune the fragrances. There is at least one theory that says that if a specific aroma really turns you off, you don't need the oil — your body is telling you something.

3. Finally, you can blend fragrances for perfumery effect alone. The soap industry giants pay a lot of money to develop a fragrance that is widely attractive and distinctive. You can do this yourself using essential oils, fragrance oils or combinations of both. It would be rather costly to make up a batch of soap every time you wanted to try out a new fragrance combination. Try this: Place a differently scented drop of oil on one of several cotton swabs and then bundle swabs with different fragrances in a plastic bag and test their fragrance; then try a different grouping of swabs. The final fragrance will be subtly different when the scents are actually blended together, but you can make an excellent approximation.

There are two more secrets to evaluating blends. First, blended fragrances age and change subtly. To approximate this change, put the bundle of swabs in a zip-lock bag and test the fragrance again after a day. This will more closely approximate the ultimate fragrance that is developed. Second, few perfumes are equal blends; complex blends are developed by using multiple swabs for the primary fragrance and fewer swabs for minor components.

FRAGRANCE "NOTES"

For a variety of reasons, good perfumes are a balanced blend of fragrances. Each aroma has a certain characteristic, usually called a "note." The notes, indeed, are like music and blending is like composing. In music, you might choose a major or minor key; in fragrances that would be woodsy, floral or exotic. In piano or orchestral music, a composer does not just compose for the right hand or just for the piccolo. He seeks a balance of highs and

How do you develop a fragrance? In perfumery, balance generally is the key. First you pick a theme. You might want a woodsy outdoor aroma, a light floral aroma or an exotic romantic aroma. Once you select your theme, read the descriptions of the fragrances (pages 122 to 133) Which oils are floral, woodsy or earthy, or exotic? If you have a wide selection of oils and fragrances to choose from, write down your reactions to them and evaluate their scents. How do they fit into the category you are looking for?

lows, piccolo and French horn, tuba, violin and viola, and bass fiddle. Similarly, in fragrance blending, there are base notes, middle notes and top notes. And a balanced blend generally represents all three types of fragrance notes.

Base Notes are full, rich, earthy aromas that usually serve to anchor a blend. Many of the wood oils are base notes, like guaiac and cinnamon and vetiver. Their components often are less volatile and they seem to cause the more volatile lighter notes to remain along with them.

Top Notes are light, volatile and frequently sweet — something we might call pure and fresh, such as juniper, mint and various citrus oils.

And finally, *Middle Notes*, which are just in-between. Frequently we call these middle notes as tending to top or tending to base. Lemongrass, pine and lily of the valley all are examples of middle notes. And rose. Actually, rose is a special case for many reasons. It is healing of mind and body, heart and soul. It frequently is considered a blended fragrance all by itself, with elements of base, middle and top notes together in its fragrance. Rose is considered the perfect all-around oil except for its rarity, and hence, its cost. ... Ouch!

FRAGRANCE BLENDING

Fragrance blending is a highly personal and subjective area. You can choose herbs and essential oils for their aromatherapy values or use what you like for a personal statement. We suggest starting with about 10ml (2 teaspoons) of essential oil per 1kg (2.2 pounds) of oil, increasing according to your desired scent to about three times that level. Remember, the finished soap will be less fragrant than your raw soap stock which is probably still warm, so the addition of twice the amount of fragrance oil will not double the fragrance.

It also is important to note that single-ingredient fragrances are more "effective" than blends. That is, 30ml (1 ounce) of lavender essential oil in 4.5kg (10 pounds) of soap may produce a fully acceptable level of fragrance. However, a lavender/rosemary/lemon blend may require at least 45ml (1.5 total ounces) of essential oil to produce a fragrance of similar intensity. Presumably, it is related to the olfactory detection level of the chemical constituents of the individual oils. In music, this would be equivalent to saying that an orchestra is no louder than the volume of any instrument. This is not true in sound, but does appear true in fragrance terms.

Many people approach fragrance blending as a science, selecting three oils to represent each of the three types of notes — top, middle and base. This is fine, but remember that top notes are more volatile, fleeting and light than middle and base notes. It is advisable to physically add more of the oils representing top notes. Similarly, base notes not only are less volatile; they are frequently stronger, lingering longer than the others. Base notes should represent the smallest volume added to your fragrance blend.

PERFUME BLENDS

When creating a custom scent for soap, take a page from the perfumers' book. Perfume blends are classified based on their fragrance profiles. It would be a mistake to think that all perfumes fall into one specific category, as there are numerous crossovers that blend floral with green or woodsy characteristics. However, the following are accepted categories and they are listed together with a few of the more famous perfumes of that type.

- Floral perfumes have one or more flowers (often rose, though hyacinth is frequently used) as the dominant note or theme. Diamonds and Sapphires, White Linen, and Anais Anais all represent variations of floral types. Chanel No. 5, Rive Gauche, Arpege and Mme. Rochas represent additional members of this family in the French tradition, sometimes called a floral/aldehydic type.

- Ambery fragrances may feature vanilla, musks and a variety of flower and woodsy materials. We often call these perfumes full-bodied or heavy — reminiscent of the Victorian era. Shalimar and Opium are among the better known in this category.

- Woodsy perfumes usually contain or are reminiscent of sandalwood or cedar, and often have a background of patchouli. Chanel No. 19 and Safari are representative members of this family.

- Leather perfumes usually feature scents of honey, tobacco and various woods. Think English Leather as one of the first in this category.

- Chypre means Cyprus and this class of perfumes is named for a Coty® perfume. Bergamot, oak moss, patchouli and labdanum are components of this type of fragrance — usually designed for men. Lighter blends in this class often are called green. CK1 and Charlie are perfumes in this category.

- Fougere, usually based on lavender, oak moss and coumarin, is another class of scents typically designed for men and characterized by a herbaceous, woodsy aroma. Canon, Brut and Drakkar Noir represent variations on this theme.

- Citrus or fruity fragrances have emerged as major fragrances, often due to the availability of newer synthetic fragrance compounds for blending.

- Oceanic fragrances incorporate both flower (lily and peony) and "oceanic" notes coming from lichen, broom and amber. Dune was one of the first in this category.

- Unami is a final family of fragrances built around synthetic components resembling food flavors; these often contain vanilla, which tends to be a flavor and fragrance enhancer.

FRAGRANCE AND YOUR PERSONALITY

What does your choice of fragrance say about you? Do you always wear the same fragrance or do you change your perfume as you change your mood? Here are a few personality traits and their perceived fragrance attraction.

- Active optimistic women: Spring floral notes such as lily of the valley and freesia.
- Young women who enjoy solitude (are there any?): Oriental sweet fragrances.
- Extroverted, impulsive or spontaneous: Fresh florals with notes of fruit.
- Emotionally stable, extroverted women: Chypre fragrances with oak moss and bergamot.

Fragrance choice can be a matter of personality and personal preference, or it can be strictly a matter of business. Fragrance sellers want to provide a wide range of options to attract the largest set of customers. Buyers want fragrances that are stable in their products and which are real, relevant, trendy, traditional and, above all, attractive to customers. It is counter-productive to make soap redolent with patchouli, which may be your own personal favorite, if patchouli drives a significant number of patrons from your store or booth. We would think that we all have experienced a store where the fragrance level assaulted us from all sides and jarred us to the bone. This reminds Bob of his youth when his grandmother would send letters and cards saturated with sachet. One of her cards sent him to the back porch where he would carefully shake out the sachet and air out the card until he felt it was "safe" to read.

Selling soap to the public means pleasing the public first and this may go completely against your personal preferences. *Remember, it is not good business to ignore your clientele.* With this in mind, we turned to our old friends who manage soap-making businesses, to see what fragrances are hot. We asked Amber at Bramble Berry, Melody at Rainbow Meadow and Trina at Snowdrift Farm what was HOT in their end of the business. These wonderful women wrote back and gave us their list of best-sellers — some were hot and trendy and others were always in vogue, year after year.

Amber (one of Katherine's favorite fragrances, by the way) said her favorite fragrance was an oatmeal-milk and honey fragrance, with lavender essential oil a perennial second. These were followed by "Energy," vanilla select, lavender fragrance oil, white tea and ginger and sandalwood. We would classify these as homey, floral and exotic or oriental in type. Amber also allowed us in on her projections for up and coming fragrances. She predicts Kumquat (fruity, green notes, fun and uplifting); Wasabi (an amazing blend embracing eucalyptus, ginger, thyme, amber and musk for a thoroughly rounded fragrance); and a blend called Basmati Rice that embraces peach, strawberry, lemon, rose, lily of the valley and cedar wood with a bit of spice and vanilla in the base. Keep your eyes (and nose) on these comers.

Melody only sells essential oils and lists her best-sellers in order: lavender, bitter almond, eucalyptus, grapefruit, rosemary, peppermint, spearmint, tea tree, lemon and tangerine. Here we see a heavy leaning toward the herbal and citrus fragrances.

Finally, Trina says that her truly hot fragrances are Satsuma (sweet orange type), Lavender Fields, Chocolover's, Citrus & Sage, Green Tea and Plumeria, which are flying off the shelf along with designer perfume-type fragrances. Top-selling fragrances in this category are similar to Vera Wang's Princess, Acqua di Gio (Armani type) and Pleasure's Delight (Estee Lauder type).

There you are — the top traditional fragrances, long-term best-sellers and hot new scents. Try them. You'll love them! And, if you have never tried amber, try some now. Amber is prepared through a process of destructively heating gem-type amber and collecting the volatile oils, often by admixing with jojoba wax. Katherine personally feels that it has a heavenly, haunting, uplifting aroma … just her opinion.

See Chapter 14 for a list of fragrance and aromatherapy properties and blending suggestions for essential oils used —or occasionally avoided — in soap making.

Chapter Seven

NO-LYE SOAP MAKING: MELT-AND-POUR & REBATCHING

There is something inherently satisfying about making soap. Maybe it relates to the 4,500-plus years' history of human soap making or maybe it simply reflects our desire to keep the jungle at bay and put our stamp on our personal environment. For pioneer women, soap making was an annual event, often lasting days while lye was leached from wood ashes saved from the winter fires and then cooked with fat as the spring thaw began.

Today, soap making is much simpler and there are four main options available: melt-and-pour (M&P), rebatching, cold process and the traditional hot or boiled process. Melt-and-pour is the easiest and involves doing just what it sounds like — melting and pouring. Rebatching is a tiny bit more complicated and is discussed following the section on M&P.

For those of us with the creative urge to hand-make something a cut above the mass-produced — something milder and more moisturizing — luxurious — something that exactly fits our conception of soapiness while avoiding the chemical hazards of saponification — there is a way. Or more precisely, there are two ways: No. 1) melt-and-pour and No. 2) rebatched, often called hand-milled soaps. Both melt-and-pour and rebatched soaps start with pre-made soap that can be easily purchased and ready to use.

MELT-AND-POUR

Melt-and-pour soap (often called M&P) is made with special, and usually secret, ingredients that allow it to easily melt in a microwave oven or in a pan of hot water so you can add your own special ingredients and let it solidify again. Melt-and-pour base soap is readily available in both transparent and opaque white and can be purchased by the pound at various hobby stores and discount department stores. It is very easy to use and is suitable for

simple kids' projects, requiring the same sort of supervision necessary for baking cookies.

Other than its ease of use, the major advantage of melt-and-pour soap is the ability to produce striking visual effects by layering and embedding different colors and objects. This is the easiest soap to use for layering. The major disadvantage is not knowing anything about the basic soap ingredients, since some melt-and-pours contain various organic solvents and chemicals that enable them to re-melt. It is, however, the best soap for kids' projects and its transparency allows for enormous creativity in design. Many professional home soap makers use melt-and-pour exclusively.

MELT-AND-POUR MAGIC

For melt-and-pour soap making, the necessary equipment is simple: melt-and-pour soap base, a heat-resistant container (usually glass) for melting the soap, a mold (usually plastic) for the finished soap, color and fragrance, and a pan of hot water into which water and the glass container can be placed. (A microwave oven can be used in place of the pan of water.)

You can find a wide variety of molds that can be used for all types of soap. Candy molds — available at virtually any craft or hobby shop — can produce small fancy soaps for the powder room. Round, rectangular and fancy shapes also are available in many craft stores and from soap suppliers (see Resources, page 149) by mail or Internet order. Clean, dry plastic molds are the best for this type of soap since the flexibility of plastic makes it much easier to remove the finished soap from the mold. However, the silicone baking molds in pan or loaf shape are extremely simple to use and are very durable.

Clear colorless melt-and-pour base comes in a variety of shapes and is easy to cut into manageable pieces.

All the equipment needed for making melt-and-pour soap. If you use a microwave oven, you don't even need the pan.

Just a few of the many color concentrates available for melt-and-pour: yellow, green, blue and shocking pink. Color concentrates can be mixed to produce other shades.

Food, Drug & Cosmetic (FD&C) use approved dyes are the colorants of choice for melt-and-pour soap. Powdered dyes are available for large batches of soap, but the most convenient forms to use are dye concentrates, usually called color tabs or color nuggets, where the color has been partially diluted in a melt-and-pour soap base. Each supplier offers his own suggestions as to how much to use for 454g (1 pound) of soap, depending on the depth of color desired. Treat these suggestions as starting points; your preference may demand the use of more or less colorant to reach your own desired level of color.

The final optional ingredient is fragrance. Essential oils derived from herbs and flowers usually are available from health and nutrition stores as well as from soap and aromatherapy suppliers. Fragrance oils are available from many of the same sources. A good starting point for scent addition is 2.5ml (0.5 teaspoon) of essential oil or 5ml (1 teaspoon) of fragrance oil per 454g (1 pound) of soap, added to the melted soap just before pouring it into the mold.

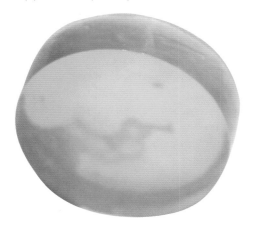

Finished bar of melt-and-pour soap with color and scent.

MELT-AND-POUR IN THE MICROWAVE

Yield: 118ml to 236ml (4- to 8-ounce) batch of soap (1 to 3 bars)

INSTRUCTIONS

1. Slice a piece of melt-and-pour base soap into approximately 1.2cm to 2.5cm (0.5" to 1") cubes, and place them in the glass container.

2. Slice a piece of soap color and add it to the container with the soap.

3. Heat the soap on full power for 30 seconds and then check to see if it is completely melted. Repeat until the soap is completely liquefied (melted).

4. Add the desired amount of fragrance oil and stir.

5. If you want your soap to be a uniform color, stir the soap with a spoon or small whisk until the color is even. (For other color effects, see the following section on personalizing your soap.)

6. Carefully pour the soap into the mold and leave at room temperature for an hour or until solid.

7. Turn the mold upside down and gently twist or push on the bottom to release the soap. If the soap does not come out easily, refrigerate or freeze for an hour and try again. You also can pour a little warm water on the inverted mold (or dip the mold briefly in a pan of warm water) to help the soap slide out of the mold.

8. Immediately wrap the finished soap in plastic wrap or place it in a plastic bag or similar container. Left open, it will pick up moisture from the air and become cloudy over time.

Ready for the microwave; it only takes a few 30-second bursts on full power to melt.

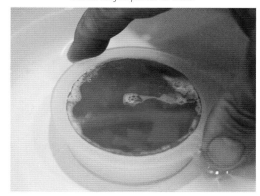

Place the filled mold in warm water to loosen the soap.

Gently warmed, the soap pops out of the mold with minimum effort.

MAKING IT PERSONAL: FRAGRANCE, COLOR AND STYLE WITH MELT-AND-POUR

Melt-and-pour soap lends itself to creative visual techniques because it is transparent and, through the use of dyes, striking colors can be achieved. Even the pigment colors commonly preferred for cold-process soap can be used to give interesting effects, though much of the brilliance of the color is lost.

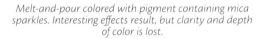

Melt-and-pour colored with pigment containing mica sparkles. Interesting effects result, but clarity and depth of color is lost.

When you add scent, you add another dimension to your creation. Since it is so very easy to handle melt-and-pour, you can blend colors, scents and visual effects with striking results. Pouring a layer of one color and letting the layer cool until it thickens (normally 5 to 10 minutes) then pouring a second layer of a different color (and scent) will produce a layered soap. This process can be repeated to form a series of colored layers.

The first layer is not ordinarily allowed to completely solidify or the different layers may not stick together in the finished soap. If the layers don't stick together sufficiently, a small amount of alcohol (grain or rubbing alcohol) can be sprayed or brushed on the surface of the first layer prior to pouring subsequent layers to help the layers stick together.

There are many ways to get special visual effects by partially mixing colors.

Adding a small amount of a darker colored soap to the initial melted soap and dragging the color through with a fork, chopstick or small whisk will create swirls and marble effects. The extent of the effect can be varied. Form subsequent layers without allowing the initial layers to thicken appreciably, and then partially mix the layers.

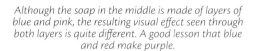

Although the soap in the middle is made of layers of blue and pink, the resulting visual effect seen through both layers is quite different. A good lesson that blue and red make purple.

Variegated soaps can also be made by forming cubes of colored soap, thoroughly chilling them so they don't melt appreciably when hot soap is poured over them, and embedding them in a mold full of clear melt-and-pour. The embedded soap does not have to be melt-and-pour; any colored soap can be used. In fact, the primary difficulty with embedding melt-and-pour soap is the tendency of the imbedded soap to partially melt into the surrounding soap. However, since cold-process soap resists melting, it often is easier to use chunks of ordinary cold-process soaps to create these effects.

Variegated colors result from mixing types and colors of soap. Cold-process soap can be added through melt-and-pour or just placed in the middle, between layers.

First, a thin layer of soap is poured and allowed to thicken.

The filled mold is ready to release the soap.

Chunks of opaque soap are scattered atop the first layer and gently pressed into the bottom layer.

The finished soap.

Additional melt-and-pour is poured on top to completely fill the mold.

Three types of objects embedded: a plastic fly, seashells and a large irregular chunk of clear melt-and-pour.

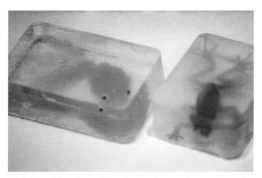

A fish and frog in melt-and-pour. Remember to place the objects upside down in the mold, as the smoothest (top) side of the soap will be against the bottom of the mold.

Kids of all ages love matching fragrances to selected colors: lemon yellow, mint green, blueberry and strawberry.

Using a cookie cutter to cut a figure out of dark soap, and then embedding this chilled figure into the center of a clear melt-and-pour bar can produce another interesting effect. Depending on the melting temperature of the soap, it may be necessary to chill the imbedded soap in the freezer prior to using to avoid appreciable melting. When you are forming layers, freezing one layer will not permit good adhesion with the next layer. You also can take advantage of another feature of the various melt-and-pour soap bases, as the more transparent soaps are softer than the translucent varieties. Thus, you can use a lower-melting transparent soap in combination with a more colored and harder translucent soap to avoid intermingling the colors.

You can avoid the melting issue altogether by embedding seashells or flat rubber toys. The only problem in handling small rubber toys is that they may try to float to the top of the mold instead of staying where you want them. If this happens, use a toothpick to push the toy back to the center of the mold until the melt-and-pour hardens enough to trap it where you want it. Seashells are easier to handle and usually heavy enough so they don't float. In all cases where toys are used in soap — remember — *they can be a choking hazard for small children.*

Multi-layered soaps can also be made more interesting by the judicious combination of fragrances, especially those reflecting the color selection. Layers of pink strawberry or raspberry alternating with creamy vanilla or dark chocolate; a red cherry layer on top of a white chocolate layer; a layer of violet lavender over a pinkish rose — all are examples of fragrance combinations reinforcing the visual impact. Although the same approach could be taken with chunks of one fragrance embedded in another, the fragrance of the smaller pieces often will get lost and, in that case, it is often more effective to combine the fragrances rather than to keep them separate.

REBATCHED SOAP

Rebatched soap is an easy-to-use form of cold-process soap. In fact, rebatching starts with cold-process soap that is only a day or two old (having been sealed in plastic bags) and still fresh enough to retain a high water content. This new soap is shredded or extruded into what typically are called soap noodles. Although some soap makers rebatch all their cold-process soap, many simply buy the packaged noodles from a supplier.

These soap noodles usually are high in olive oil and have not been left in the open to cure and lose moisture. Instead, usually within 24 hours of saponification, the soap is grated, extruded in a meat grinder or chopped in a food mill and immediately placed in a plastic bag to prevent water loss and retain the initial plasticity of the soap.

The base often is available in a variety of raw ingredients: 100-percent olive oil, mostly olive oil, lard and coconut blends, etc. The soap maker can make a variety of soaps without having to handle lye at all. An additional advantage of rebatching is the ability to make or buy large batches of cold-process soap and convert it into many special colors, scents, shapes, etc. — something that often is difficult to do directly with a large batch of cold-process soap. The process of rebatching soap requires adding water, or more typically milk, to the noodles and heating the mixture to about the boiling point of water to redissolve the soap. Soap can be rebatched in a crockpot, double boiler or in a covered casserole dish using a microwave or conventional oven.

Many of the same decorative techniques used for melt-and-pour soaps can be applied to rebatched or hand-milled soaps. When the soap is completely melted, oils, fragrances, herbs and color can be added before the soap is put into a mold to harden.

Color effects can be varied with rebatched soap, depending on when the color is added.

WHY REBATCH?

Since the soap is already made, you do not have to handle lye. Furthermore, you can add ingredients that are not stable under the highly alkaline conditions present during the initial soap-making process. Several FD&C dyes actually will give different colors when used in M&P or rebatched soap.

For those wanting to produce soap using aromatherapy essential oils, rebatched soap will retain all essential oil components except those that are not stable to, or able to evaporate at, the temperatures required to melt the soap. Herbs also may be added to the melted soap with substantially less discoloration than when added to cold- or hot-processed soap. Milk is easier to use in this process than water which makes rebatching a very simple way to make goat's

Soap noodles can be easily rebatched in a casserole dish.

milk soap, noted for its silky feel. In general, whole milk from any source, or fresh or reconstituted powdered milk will more easily dissolve the soap noodles than reduced-fat milk, which in turn will work better than plain water. Typically, when you purchase soap designed for rebatching, the supplier will offer instructions for the appropriate temperature and amount of liquid to add to their particular recipe.

GENERAL DIRECTIONS FOR REBATCHING

Soap can be rebatched in a double boiler, a crockpot set to low, or in a covered pot or dish in the oven with the oven temperature set at 200 F to 225 F (93 C to 107 C). In general, a typical starting point is to add a scant 120ml (0.5 cup) of room temperature or slightly warm whole milk to each 453g (1 pound) of fresh soap noodles, or your own freshly made and ground cold-process soap. To give you a feel for volumes, a 2L (2-quart) covered casserole will hold approximately 1.1kg (2.5 pounds) of soap noodles and 300ml (1.25 cups) of whole milk with sufficient room to add additional liquid if needed.

REBATCHING IN A CASSEROLE DISH

Add your specific ingredients using the general directions above and cover the casserole dish. Heat this mixture at 220 F to 250 F (93 C to 107 C) for one to three hours to produce a thick soap "soup." The mixture is not always smooth at this point; a little mixing with a small whisk or hand blender can help the melting process and form a uniform soup. If the soap still is not dissolving or melting, add another 120ml (0.5 cup) of warm milk or water for each 453g (1 pound) of soap noodles. Be careful not to add too much liquid or it will take much longer for the soap to sufficiently solidify to be removed from the mold.

To speed up the process, stir the soap mixture by hand as the soap is melting.

Blend in additional color at any stage in the process.

When the thick rebatched soap has melted to the point where it has no obvious solid chunks remaining, add colorants, fragrances, and special oils or ground herbs and mix well. A good starting point for adding scent is 15ml (0.5 ounce) of essential oil or 30ml to 60ml (1 to 2 ounces) of fragrance oil for every 1kg to 1.5kg (2 to 3 pounds) soap noodles. Pour the soap into a mold.

NOTE

Due to the high temperatures involved in this process, some fragrance will be lost to evaporation (the lighter the fragrance, the more will be lost).

REBATCHING IN THE MICROWAVE

We have found that a very simple way to make small batches, up to 906g (2 pounds), of rebatched soap is in the microwave oven. Place 453g to 680g (1 to 1.5 pounds) of soap noodles in a small glass casserole dish and add 120ml (0.5 cup) of tepid whole milk. Cover the dish and place it in the microwave. Heat on full power for 60 seconds and then examine the contents to see how far the soap has melted.

Continue to heat in 60-second intervals until an appreciable amount of the soap has melted, then add coloring and use a fork to stir the soap (to help it melt uniformly). Continue heating in 60-second cycles and add about 15ml (1 tablespoon) of milk between cycles until the soap is a uniform consistency — usually more "spoonable" than pourable. When the soap has reached a uniform stage (thick, but spoonable) stir in about 5ml (1 teaspoon) of your desired fragrance oil and use a spoon, ladle or rubber kitchen spatula to transfer your newly scented soap into a mold.

This rebatched soap is thick enough to use a rubber spatula to fill the molds.

As an alternative to using a mold, you can easily roll bits of soap in your hands as the rebatched soap cools down to make soap balls. If you wet your hands, the soap will not be as sticky. The soap balls tend to collapse a bit as they cool and age; you can re-roll them in your hands after a few hours to help retain their round shape.

When the rebatched soap is cool, wet your hands and roll into balls.

Re-roll the soap ball to keep it round if it becomes deformed.

NOTE

Microwave ovens vary in power or strength; you must gauge the length of cooking time for your particular oven.

Soap rebatched this way normally will be ready to remove from the mold in six to 12 hours. Larger batches, which are thinner due to the addition of extra milk, may take as long as a few days to sufficiently solidify and be safely removed from the mold. Often it is helpful to freeze the poured mold first to make unmolding easier. It is important to lightly press on the soap (poke it gently) to determine that it is solid enough to hold its shape when removed from the mold. Although rebatched soap does not need to cure (there is no unreacted lye or incomplete chemical reaction in the soap), it still needs to "rest" in the open air for three to five weeks so any excess water evaporates and the soap hardens to a usable state. If used prematurely, the rebatched soap has a tendency to dissolve too quickly in water.

Frozen soap in a mold is warmed in a bowl of hot water.

Chocolate-scented soap with coconut-scented white and dark soap as "frosting."

After 10 to 15 seconds in hot water, the soap easily comes out of the mold.

Layered soap formed by dividing the soap batch and using different colors. You don't have to scent the layers differently, although that adds to the "scentsation."

LAYERING REBATCHED SOAP

Like melt-and-pour, rebatched soap can be formed into layers, though the effect may not be as striking as with melt-and-pour soaps. To layer rebatched soap, simply fill half the mold with the original layer and as soon as this layer has thickened to where it is soft but solid, add the second layer. Alternately, contrasting colored and scented soap can be spread or dribbled on top of the original batch of soap, in a fashion similar to frosting a cake.

Color uniformity in rebatched soaps can vary with the type of colorant used and when it is added. Adding water-soluble dyes to the milk or water prior to starting rebatching, ordinarily will produce a uniform color. If you use any of the various color tabs — a concentrate of soap and dye — you can achieve a marbleized effect by adding the color tab when the soap is nearly dissolved, but still thick. The earlier a color tab is added, the more uniform the color will be. We must also point out that color often intensifies in rebatched soap, especially when color tabs are used. So don't be surprised when that pale lavender becomes darker in a day or two.

Although the rebatching technique also can be used to recover batches of cold-process soaps that are cosmetically challenged (ugly), or don't have the desired fragrance, many people routinely rebatch almost all their handmade soap. Some prefer the texture of rebatched soap which has the smooth hand feel of gelled soap, while others want to be absolutely certain that all the ingredients are thoroughly reacted. In any case, though some soap makers may refer to rebatching as something done to save a batch of soap and hand milling as an intentional or planned operation, the distinction has no basis. In fact — either term may be used — no matter what the original intentions were.

When color is added just before transferring the soap into a mold, the color usually comes out in streaks and swirls; when added from the beginning, a more uniform color results.

— Chapter Eight —
COLD-PROCESS SOAP MAKING

Cold-process soap offers a great deal of flexibility in the selection and use of fats and oils, colorants and fragrances. It is the principle process used to make soap at home for those very reasons. There are dangers, of course. Lye, an essential chemical part for converting fat or oil to soap, is extremely hazardous, corrosive and poisonous. Making soap "from scratch" with children, animals and spouses underfoot is not appropriate for most people.

Saponification, the chemical process that converts oils and fats to soap, requires simple but special equipment to measure ingredients and contain the reacting ingredients, as well as specific personal equipment to assure the safety of the soap maker and family.

When you are ready to make your soap, first select your recipe (see pages 102 to 120). Typos do happen and most information on the Internet is unchecked, so recheck the proportions before beginning. You can easily access a lye calculator online, which will allow you to enter the weight of ingredients while the amount of lye required is automatically calculated. Assemble all of your ingredients for the recipe you've chosen, clean and prepare your molds and put on your protective clothing. We strongly suggest you wear gloves and eye protection such as safety glasses or goggles (not contact lenses).

THE COLD PROCESS

In the cold process, the oil is first heated to the desired temperature. Once the lye and water mixture is added, no further heating is needed. The chemical reaction of saponification proceeds and it continues to generate sufficient heat until the thickened soap stock is ready to be poured into molds to solidify. During the initial stages, the temperature of the mixture normally falls to around room temperature and seldom generates significant heat unless the thickened soap is poured into a large mold, at which time the internal heat will cause the mixture to gel. In this regard, cold-process soap that reaches the gel stage has the finished look and feel of hot-process soap. If smaller molds are used under cold-process conditions, heat loss to the atmosphere dominates and the soap never reaches the gel stage. The result is soap with a different texture. The small crystals and spaces between the crystals (formed as the water evaporates) are evident. The preference for a smooth plastic-type (gelled) or a more crystalline bar is intensely personal since

both types are fully finished and functional. It is a worthwhile experience to try different conditions and produce different types of soap. You may not change your preference, but you will learn how to control the overall appearance of the finished product and that in itself is a worthwhile endeavor.

PROCEDURE

1. Choose your desired recipe.

2. Have your molds prepared ahead of time and lay them out where you intend to fill them. Once the soap gets thick, you will not have time to clean and dry them. Most molds can be cleaned with dish soap, water and a little elbow grease.

3. Weigh out the appropriate amounts of fat and oil and transfer them to your soap pot.

4. Mix the fats and oils and heat to about 122 F to 140 F (50 C to 60 C). Remove from the heat.

5. Measure the water (distilled or deionized) and place in the container used for the lye solution.

6. In a well-ventilated area, weigh the lye and carefully pour it in the water. Mix this solution outside or on the stove top with an adequate vent fan running. When stirring, use gloves and eye protection!

Carefully stir the water as you are adding solid lye. Without stirring, the lye tends to form a crusty solid that's hard to safely break up once formed.

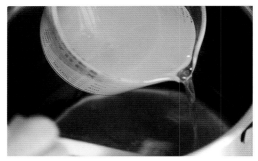

Carefully add the lye solution to the heated oils taking care to avoid splashing.

When the lye solution turns clear, it is ready to go.

7. When the lye is completely dissolved and the solution clear, stir it into the warm oil. This can be done fairly rapidly, taking care to avoid splashing. Very soon the oil will become murky from the soap crystals that are forming. Keep stirring and the oil will become opaque and finally thicken into a custard-like consistency.

8. The soap is ready to scent or mold when the oil and lye phases no longer separate and you can form a "trace" on the surface. Ordinarily this step takes about 30 minutes but it can take as long as four hours with ordinary stirring, depending on conditions. If it is not thickening, check the temperature. If the temperature has dropped below 100 F (38 C), gently reheat the pot on the stove to about 120 F (49 C). If you have a stick blender available, several 10- to 20-second pulses usually serve to thicken the batch.

TRACE

Trace: The point at which a batch of soap is thick enough to pour into molds; when is is thick enough to resist separating back into oil and water layers. Trace is the point when a spoonful of the mixture, poured back into the pot, leaves a brief, faint imprint on the surface.

As the reaction proceeds, the soap visibly thickens. You will be able to feel as well as see the difference.

When the soap is thickened, add fragrance, herbs, colorants, etc. with good agitation. You may want to use a stainless steel whisk to disperse solids such as clay, ground oatmeal, ground herbs or pigments.

Add essential oils by the spoonful.

9. Pour the thickened soap into molds. Leave the molds in a warm place 70 F to 80 F (21 C to 27 C), for one to two days. This allows the saponification reaction to continue until complete and for the bars to harden and maintain their shape. If you are using large flat molds 20cm by 20cm (8" by 8") or larger, you usually will be able to see the soap become translucent after an hour or less. This is the gel phase and is a sign that the soap will have a smooth and pliable interior as it comes from the mold.

A ladle is a handy tool for transferring your soap mixture into the mold.

Small, individual soap molds will not go through this stage, but will make perfectly fine, usable soap just the same. However, it probably will be more difficult to cut without crumbling. Using smaller molds generally eliminates the necessity to cut the bars into smaller pieces.

Once the soap is in the mold, it will take a few hours to solidify. It still is very soft at this point.

10. When using hard plastic molds, freeze the molds for three to eight hours or overnight. Soap in plastic molds can be removed by heating the bottom in hot tap water for several seconds. PVC pipe molds may take a little longer and a hair dryer may be a better choice to gently heat the exterior of this mold. Invert and gently push on the bottom to release the soap. If you need to push hard on the soap to extricate it from the mold, place the metal top of an orange juice can against the surface of the soap and push against it with a thick wooden dowel.

Dip the bottom of the mold in warm water for five to 10 seconds to loosen the soap.

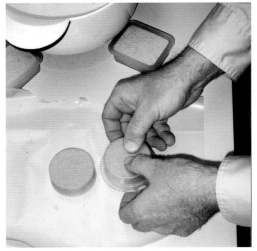

Once the soap is loose, push the bottom and flex the mold like an ice cube tray and pop the soap out.

11. Cut the soap to size if necessary. Soap that has gone through the gel phase generally can be easily cut with a sharp, thin knife such as a boning knife. A thin wire such as a cheese cutter, clay slicer, guitar string or piano wire works if you can keep it taut. If you intend to make soap on a large scale, a jigsaw or band saw also will work (use a blade designed to cut plastic).

A band saw easily cuts through the pumice soap in paper milk cartons. The speed of the saw helps eliminate crumbling of the soap.

12. Rest the soap on waxed or butcher's paper until it is firm, usually one to two days. (Your touch should not leave an indentation in the soap.)

Chapter Eight: Cold-Process Soap Making

13. Move the soap to storage but allow for plenty of air circulation around the bars. After about two to four weeks, examine the soap for light(er) surfaces. This might indicate the presence of sodium carbonate, formed if unreacted lye comes into contact with carbon dioxide from the air. This material should be scraped off and discarded or, better yet, saved for the laundry. On the other hand, a whitish surface often is common with cold-process soaps and often indicates that rapid surface crystallization has caused a different type of soap crystal to form on the cooler surface. This material is indistinguishable from the interior soap and is simply a cosmetic issue. Remove it by abrasion or wipe it off with a damp towel if it is objectionable.

14. Wrap your cured soap in plastic and/or store in a plastic shoe or sweater box. All are suitable for storage.

The hard work is done! The soap is ready to be cured and dried for three to five weeks.

CLEANING UP

Sooner or later it happens to the best of us. You have your soap in molds and a stack of dirty pots and utensils in the sink. What now? First of all, soap is not the only thing covering all those surfaces. The pH still is very high, it still can cause burns, and it will laugh at water. In fact, it will coat everything it touches with an oily layer. You might want to wait overnight to let chemistry complete the soap transformation and then it will be easier to clean in the morning. We also found that cleanup is much faster if you pour some liquid dish soap directly onto the equipment coated with soap. Let it sit for 10 to 15 minutes and then gently scrub to work up a good lather. The thick lather can then be washed off with water. Be sure to wear gloves.

If you have a septic tank, we strongly suggest you scrape as much residual soap as possible out of the pot and off the utensils and put the scrapings in the garbage. You don't want to damage your septic field or plug up the drains. If you need to clean up right away, *keep your gloves on.* You can use a little vinegar to cut the pH to a safer level. Scrub with a lot of soap or detergent and a brush, rinsing several times along the way to remove oily water. You also can put the items in the dishwasher, since dishwasher detergent is very high in alkali (so high that dishwashers can't have aluminum parts exposed). If you do use the dishwasher, run everything through *twice.*

Dirty equipment is easier to clean after 24 hours when the oils have mostly converted into soap. Fresh soap residue is quite oily and hard to clean.

TROUBLESHOOTING

Here are a few of the most common problems encountered with cold-process soap making.

1. My soap won't trace. What can I do?
This usually happens when making nearly 100-percent olive oil soaps, which can take hours (and sometimes days) to trace. Maintain a reasonable temperature and agitate the mixture periodically. It will slowly solidify. If you aren't making a high olive oil soap, check your ingredients to be sure you added the correct amount of lye. Insufficient lye is another possible cause, so re-check your recipes to make sure the correct amount of lye was specified.

2. The soap traced but turned to liquid once I put it in the mold.
This probably is an example of a false trace. False trace usually happens when the reaction temperature drops low enough to let the solid fats or oils solidify before they saponify. Put the mixture back in the soap pot and reheat while stirring until it traces again. Next time you make this soap, check your starting temperatures.

3. The soap traced, but once it was placed in the mold a thin oily layer formed on top.
This probably is your essential or fragrance oil separating out. It normally will be re-absorbed into the soap, so just wait a day or so.

4. The top of the soap turned into a white powder.
The white powder generally is just a different type of soap crystal. The most common solution is to scrape it off. Next time, try covering the exposed surface of the soap (in the mold) with plastic wrap.

5. During (or after) curing, I noticed brown or orange spots on the surface of the soap.
Those dreaded orange spots are usually from oxidation of excess oils. Reduce your superfat level or add an antioxidant to the soap during saponification.

6. When I was taking my soap out of the molds, I noticed a liquid layer at the bottom.
This layer, usually brownish, generally is caused when the lye solution separates from the soap. Check your weights to be sure you didn't add too much lye (or too little oil). It is best to discard the entire soap batch when this happens.

7. I was just about to pour my soap into the mold when I realized I forgot to add one of the oils in the recipe.
The soap is now lye-heavy. You either can try to reheat the soap gently (to make it more liquid) and add the forgotten oil, or you could try rebatching it with the addition of the forgotten oil.

8. I tried to use my cured soap, but it was white and crumbly instead of nice and solid.
Be careful and check your ingredients. This could be an indication of too much lye. The other possibility is that you used too much solid fat or oil, which sometimes causes the soap to crack or become crumbly. A good soap usually is a balance of solid and liquid fats or oils.

9. My soap is good but the fragrance disappeared after only a few weeks.
Some fragrances are unstable or too volatile for soap making. Try a small batch with twice the amount of fragrance and see if that lasts. If not, you have just found a fragrance that is not suitable for use in cold-process soap making. You might try rebatching the non-fragrant soap and adding fragrance oil. If the fragrance is unstable to highly alkaline conditions, it likely is more stable to rebatching.

10. Everything was working fine until I added the fragrance oil at trace and the soap suddenly seemed to heat up and get solid very quickly; I could barely get it out of my pot.
You have found a fragrance oil that causes seizing. In the future, if you must use this oil, add it much earlier, at very thin trace, and be prepared to quickly put the soap in molds if it still seems to thicken too much.

11. I made some soap for gifts and now all my friends want to buy some to give as gifts.
This is not considered a problem. You friends have just discovered what you already know — the wonderful properties of handmade, handcrafted soap. Congratulations!

Chapter Eight: Cold-Process Soap Making

— Chapter Nine —

SEVEN SECRETS OF SUCCESSFUL SOAP MAKING

There are few true secrets to making good soap, though this is not always obvious to the novice. Here are some shortcuts and rules of thumb that may help a beginner gain confidence and become proficient at the many aspects of this craft.

SECRET NO. 1: PATIENCE

The first, biggest and most underrated secret is patience. We have never had a pot of "ingredients" not make soap, even if it did not quite resemble what we had in mind originally. Let us repeat that. If our recipe had the correct amount of lye and oil, we have always been able to produce good soap. This appears to be one distinct advantage of making soap at elevated starting temperatures.

When making our first several batches, we expected to finish in an hour or so, and it did not happen that way. Then we came to expect four-hour batches. Later we found that we could adjust (shorten) the time required by making slight changes in the formula — starting out at a slightly higher temperature, changing the rate of mixing, or reheating the pot when it cools off. We even poured batches into molds when the "brew" seemed nowhere near thick enough. Basically, if your proportions are correct, you can pour soap into a mold as long as it pours and the oil does not separate into a separate layer on top of the mixture when it stands without stirring. If it does separate — wait. Have patience. Wait as long as a week or two if needed. Stir it in the mold if that is possible. We have thrown away only one batch of soap — ever. For that batch, we were experimenting with new temperatures and mixing techniques and saw, too late, that it was separating as we poured it into the mold. The next day there was a fairly large soap island surrounded by liquid. After 48 hours, there was no real change except for the soap getting slicker (dare we say slimy?). For us, this soap was not worth salvaging, although we could have ground up the soap and, using the liquid, rebatched it. It was an experiment that confirmed what we had at least half expected — hot soap needs to be at full thick trace or it may separate. However, sometimes a thin top layer of oil actually is your fragrance oil separating out just a bit. When that happens, be assured that it will be drawn back into the soap as it solidifies. If you pour off the top liquid oily layer, your proportions may no longer be correct and you might be left with a large excess of lye and no way to correct it with certainty.

SECRET NO. 2: INS CALCULATION

The second very important secret, not widely known, is the use of an artificial calculation called INS to evaluate the ratio of oils in your recipe. Although we do not know what caused the original scientist to call this term "INS," it is just possible that this term reflects its relationship to its origins, since it is calculated from the Iodine Value and Saponification Value. I(odine value) 'n S(ap value). Whatever its derivation, to save you time and trouble, we have included the INS value in our table of oils.

The INS value for a mixture of oils is simply the weighted average of INS values for the mixture of oils. Most importantly, the unidentified scientist determined that the "ideal" INS average value for a fat or oil mixture for a bar of toilet soap is around 160. That innocent discovery set the wheels in motion. A quick scrutiny of our own recipes showed an INS in the near optimum range. Further calculations of many published recipes also were either in or near the ideal range. Needless to say, we adjusted our recipes and ingredients to get closer to this range. As we have said, you can make soap from almost any mixture of fats and oils, but if you want to experiment, try the INS calculation before you make your soap and see how close you are.

The INS for cottonseed oil is listed as 88, coconut oil is about 257, olive oil is about 107 and palm is 206. You can calculate that in a blend of 25 percent coconut, 25 percent cottonseed, 25 percent olive, and 25 percent palm oils. The INS factor is 164.5 ([88 + 257 +107 + 206] ÷ 4), confirming that this mixture would make a near ideal soap as far as hardness and other physical properties are concerned. This would be an excellent starting point for a soap containing cottonseed oil.

Please keep one thing in mind regarding INS. This calculation was developed based on preference panel results of people who evaluated conventional soap. Soap made from compressed soap or coconut or longer-chain fatty-acid salts without the natural glycerin, which our soaps retain.

We have an advantage from the start. The natural glycerin thickens the lather, or at least makes the tiny bubbles much more resistant to bursting and thus they are able to last longer. Think of bubble solutions purchased in a toy department. The super-sized bubbles use a soap solution that contains a high level of glycerin, which retards water evaporation and surface thinning of the bubble. Thicker bubbles naturally last longer. The glycerin also gives a different feel to the lather and leaves a softer feeling to the skin. You do not have to avoid low INS values, which, for instance, may result from all olive oil soaps. INS calculations are just a starting point, a tool that is useful when used appropriately.

SECRET NO. 3: TEMPERATURE AGITATION

The third secret is that the speed of saponification (how fast oil converts to soap) is dependent on both temperature and agitation. The reaction itself is exothermic, which means that heat is produced as the reaction proceeds. And you also need the right mixture of ingredients to really "want" to make soap. However, since oil and water do not mix, the only reaction that can take place is at the small layer where the lye solution comes into contact with the oil. Even though higher temperatures speed up the reaction, at least in the beginning, higher temperatures cause the oil and water to have less contact. To counteract this, increase agitation.

For very small batches, the blender is quite efficient; you can go from a two-phase liquid system to solid soap almost before you know it. For batches up to 4.5kg (10 pounds) or so, the stick blender is one way to speed up the process. After the lye solution is stirred into the oil for about five minutes, the stick blender can be used in cycles of 30 seconds on, 60 seconds off (to avoid overheating the blender) until trace is reached, usually within five to 10 minutes. After that, continue with regular stirring and add other ingredients as desired.

Is the stick blender a solution to all worries? No. The difficulty comes when this blender is used with blends rich in hard oils such as palm or vegetable shortening, and at low temperatures, usually around 90 F (32 C). It is possible to form a thick emulsion of oil and lye solution, rather like mayonnaise, that appears to be ready to pour into a mold. However, if the actual chemical reaction is too incomplete, saponification will proceed in the mold, generating heat as it goes. This heat can produce three results.

1. If saponification has progressed to a satisfactory point, the heat will cause the soap to go through gel phase. Many want to achieve this result, so this may not be a problem at all.

2. The melting process may have unexpected results, such as changing the color in the center of the soap. The result would be a dark, sometimes almost transparent center with normal-looking soap surrounding it. Usually, both the center and the edges of the soap will be of good quality that's quite usable, but it may not look as you intended.

3. As the soap heats up, it might separate into oil and lye solution phases that will cause the formation of lye pockets in the finished soap.

Soaps with lye pockets or layers are not safe to use. In most cases, a careful visual inspection will alert you to problems.

If the soap does not get firm, it probably under-reacted (it never got hot enough for saponification to complete). Perhaps rebatching can save this soap.

If the soap has that dark, almost translucent center, cut open a bar and examine the center. Good soap should be a nice uniform color and consistency. Pockets or layers of white, usually a crumbly material, could very easily be lye. Check the pH (using pH indicator papers available from most swimming pool supply shops) to see if it is unusually high. Lye ordinarily will give you a reading at or near 14 — extremely caustic. Check your recipe again to be sure that your calculations were correct and the proper amounts of lye and oil were used.

If the proportions were correct, rebatching might well salvage this batch too. The best thing is to simply avoid the problem in the first place. Check the temperature as you stir the oil and lye. If the temperature drops below 100 F (38 C) before the batch thickens or traces, it may be desirable to encourage saponification; gently and carefully, slightly heat the batch. If you have made this recipe before and this batch behaves significantly different than the last one, check your ingredient proportions and temperatures carefully; usually you will avoid these problems.

If you want that gelled look in your finished soap, preheat your oven to about 170 F (77 C). Put your poured (temperature-resistant) mold into the oven. Leave it at that temperature for an hour or so, or turn it off and let the temperature slowly drop over several hours. Be sure to use a cookie sheet or steel pan under the mold in case the mold warps or leaks.

SECRET NO. 4: SALVAGING A BATCH IN JEOPARDY

The fourth secret lies in accepting that sometimes your best-laid plans will go wrong at the last minute and planning ahead may salvage the batch. When you add essential oil, aloe-vera gel or herbs and other finely ground material to a warm, ready-to-pour soap batch, these ingredients, which are much cooler than the soap mixture, may cause a sudden large rise in viscosity. Viscosity tends to rise with falling temperature (i.e. gravy is thicker when it's cold than hot).

A second possible cause is due to shock crystallization. Any number of things, such as a sudden change in concentration or temperature, or a sudden addition of high surface area solids, can cause this phenomenon, which essentially is the abrupt formation of mega-scads (that's the technical term) of extremely small soap crystals (sometimes referred to as crystallites). These small crystals rub together and cause the dramatic increase in viscosity. Is this a problem? Yes, but only if the mixture gets too thick to pour into a mold — and it can. You could be stuck with a pot of soap and no way to get it out except to scoop it out and make soap balls.

As your soap-making skills increase, you will learn to recognize the warning signs of impending complications. For example, you'll recognize when the mixture has thickened to the point of tracing and is still hot. It is good to have alternative plans ready to implement. Change your plans and omit the powdered oatmeal and herbs and add only essential oils to the mixture and quickly get your molds ready. Or forget about the small fancy molds you were going to use and grab the clean, dry, quart milk cartons you have been saving for just this sort of impending disaster. Spoon the thickened soap mixture into the carton if it won't pour. Settle it by pinching the

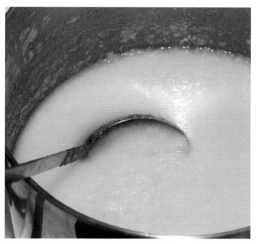

When soap reaches this stage (a consistency similar to applesauce) it is unwise to add anything that would tend to make it thicker.

As you can see by the "squiggle" on the top, this soap has or very nearly has seized.

top closed and thumping it repeatedly on the table. As another alternative, try making rebatched soap or maybe make bars by using the hydraulic mold your spouse put together for you. In this case, let the soap solidify in manageable chunks. Grate or chop it and use the result in your endeavors. Crossing your fingers or saying a prayer might help, but adding water usually does not.

But what happens if you start making your soap and the phone rings, or if it takes longer than planned and dinner is served? It doesn't matter what happens to cause an interruption — eventually it will happen. If it happens early in the soap-making process, don't worry. The oil and lye solution will separate and the reaction virtually will come to a stop except at the interface — that thin space where water and oil are in contact. During this time, the soap crystals normally will settle to the bottom of the pot. They often feel sort of grainy, like large granules, when you stir them up again. So thoroughly stir them up, reheat the pot a little if it has cooled to room temperature, and go on.

There are, of course, potential disasters that are not so easily remedied. What happens when you are looking with pride

at the solidifying soap you have just put into your mold and you realize you forgot to add 25 percent of the oils required? If your batch is still in the pot and has not reached that firm trace stage, you should be able to add the additional oils, though it would help if you could warm the forgotten oils first and then dribble them in with slow continuous stirring. The risk is that cold oil may cause shock crystallization by dropping the batch temperature, essentially seizing the batch. In any event, re-warming should be possible, but potentially tricky. In some cases, it may be simpler just to let the soap set overnight, carefully grate it (realizing that it will be very lye heavy) and then re-batch it with the missing oils as part of the rebatch.

SECRET NO. 5: IT'S NOT SET IN STONE

The fifth secret: There is no universally right set of conditions to use in soap making. The temperature of the lye solution does not have to match the temperature of the oils. There is no single best temperature to start with. When you make the same exact recipe many times, the time to trace can vary greatly. The common thread here is uncontrolled temperature variables. High temperatures (oils at 140 F [60 C], lye solution at 160 F [71 C]) are very suitable for filling small or individual molds, which rapidly lose heat once they are filled. You will need to compensate for the heat loss.

For the same reason, even though the initial temperatures are the same, a 4.5kg (10-pound) batch will get to trace faster than a 2.2kg (5-pound) batch in the same pot. Larger volumes retain more heat. Similarly, with a cluster of small molds, those in the center will remain warmer than those on the ends and, as a result, the center molds will become solid faster than those on the end.

Large flat molds generally will retain heat in the center and, depending on the temperatures, could result in a gelled center while the edges remain crystalline. Shoe-box or cubic molds probably will require lower starting temperatures and rarely need to be insulated at all. When these block-type molds are used, enough heat can be generated to not only gel the interior, but also begin boiling off the water as steam. The side effect here is that the volume can expand as well, causing the mold to overflow. This should tell you to scale up batches carefully. We would not go from a 2kg (4.5-pound) batch to a 4kg (9-pound) batch without being very cautious.

An array of molds filled with oatmeal-honey soap.

Gently press the soap surface to see if it is firm enough to remove from the mold.

SECRET NO. 6: FRAGRANCE CONCERNS

Fragrances should be added near the end of soap making, just before putting the soap into the mold. As your expertise increases, you should learn, at least in general, the chemical components of the fragrance you want to use. Most fragrance chemicals fall into one of the following chemical types: alcohols, aldehydes, ketones, esters and olefins. Chemical names don't have to be daunting and you don't have to memorize a long list of names. Look at the endings of the chemical names. Alcohols, such as the common fragrance alcohol linalool, usually end in "ol," while aldehydes usually end in "al" or even aldehyde (no one ever said chemists had to be consistent). Olefins, which are unsaturated hydrocarbons, are among the most stable fragrance compounds and usually end in "ene," as in cedrene or limonene. Esters usually have two names reflecting the alcohol and acid they came from (i.e. methyl laurate is the name of an ester).

Aldehydes and esters are common fragrance components that are unstable to basic conditions. That is, aldehydes and esters, if used to fragrance soaps, can be expected to either lose much of their aroma or change the type of aroma they generate. It is very challenging to produce a stable citrus aroma of any sort since citral, the primary essence of most citrus oils, is an aldehyde and unstable to alkali; and limonene, another major fragrance chemical component, is easily air oxidized. Benzaldehyde is the main fragrance chemical in almond extract (or synthetic almond fragrance) and maraschino cherry aroma. Benzaldehyde, obviously an aldehyde based on its name, definitely would undergo reactions if added too early in the soap-making process, though it is more stable than most aldehydes. Ketones and olefins are much more stable, but even so, they should be added just before pouring the soap into molds.

Fragrance oils should be purchased from a reputable dealer who understands soap making, since many fragrance oils (as well as a few essential oils such as cinnamon, clove, allspice and nutmeg) will accelerate saponification to the point that the entire batch can seize — thicken and turn to something similar to cottage cheese or worse — in a matter of seconds. Although several factors can cause your cold-process soap to seize, essential oils that contain significant amounts of the natural chemical compound eugenol definitely should be used with caution.

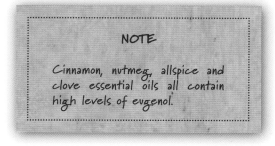

NOTE

Cinnamon, nutmeg, allspice and clove essential oils all contain high levels of eugenol.

We believe that eugenol acts as a catalyst for saponification, greatly accelerating the rate of reaction. We vividly remember one demonstration where Bob added cinnamon essential oil to soap contained in several milk carton molds. (Bob added it in the mold since he knew that this oil could cause the soap to seize. He thought he was being smart.) As we were setting up for our next demonstration, an unfamiliar sound made us look at the soap we just made. It was now steaming and beginning to foam up and out of the mold. Disaster? No, all we did was separate the soap molds and let them cool down, which eliminated the foaming.

SECRET NO. 7:
BE OBSERVANT …
YOU NEVER KNOW WHAT YOU
MIGHT DISCOVER

Soap making can be full of wonderful surprises (and a few that you really don't want to experience as well). It pays to watch your soap as you process a new recipe. When things deviate from the expected, this could be either a good or a bad thing. But follow it through to the end. For instance, during one of our first attempts at making a liquid soap product (on our own … without resorting to reading a book on the topic) we thought we would just use potassium hydroxide instead of sodium hydroxide. We also thought it might be a good idea to add some glycerin in place of part of the water since that might help keep the soap in the solution. We knew we needed to use a hot process since we hoped to make a concentrate and then dilute it down to a usable consistency. However, we were very much surprised to see our mixture turning, first transparent, and then start to solidify in our container. But the crystals or solid was translucent.

Fortunately, we had our camera handy and captured our *(mis)fortune*. It was not what we were trying to accomplish; we ruined what might have been by trying to add extra water and glycerin. We ended up with a sticky, but soft, solid transparent soap. Is this a way to make a liquid soap concentrate? Can we make a transparent soap bar? At the moment, we don't know, but the possibilities are there. We were able to dilute the sticky translucent soap to a clear amber liquid. It will take time to sort out the variables and find out exactly what we can make. For the next trial, we recommend adding little or no extra glycerin and substituting xylitol, a five-carbon sugar alcohol we found in a store specializing in natural foods.

If you want to try this for yourself, we used a ratio of 20 percent coconut oil and 80 percent canola oil. The potassium hydroxide was very nearly without discount. We had planned to make a liquid soap and adjust the pH with citric acid or possibly ascorbic acid (vitamin C). In any event, make your calculations (remember that potassium hydroxide generally is only 85 to 88 percent pure) and complete this discovery. If you perfect the process, let us know. We can always be reached through the Saponifier (*www.saponifier.com*).

This trial batch changed from clear to opaque and finally translucent.

Sticky but transparent soap made by a planned accident.

— Chapter Ten —
HOT-PROCESS SOAP MAKING

Our first excursions into hot-process soap making were adventures, revelations and definitely learning experiences. Since our ordinary cold-process conditions are actually warm, it did not appear there would be the necessity to make many alterations to our general processing techniques. So to make this book complete, we reached "outside the box" and "pushed the envelope" in order to know where problems would develop and where it would be safe to work

THE HOT PROCESS

The hot process actually refers to a variety of processes where the processing remains at a temperature significantly above room temperature. This includes the traditional, pioneer-type cooked soap, where the fat and lye and water solutions are boiled together until most of the water has evaporated and the resulting soap quickly solidifies on cooling. This type of hot process is used extensively by those involved in reenactments, Renaissance fairs and similar demonstrations of the ancient art of soap making (only the hardiest soap makers still use lye leached from ashes). Modern hot processes include "cooking" the ingredients in a crockpot or just working the ingredients at or near the boiling point of water until the mixture reaches the thick trace stage. This method offers significant advantages as well as a number of disadvantages.

OUR RESEARCH

Whenever we embark on a new process or create a new product, we first review the literature. We searched online for the various types of hot processing that we knew about: crockpot, oven "bake," pot-boiled, etc. We were, in fact, not looking for either recipes or processing conditions. We were looking for pictures. Pictures really are worth a thousand words and we were very confident that under the right processing conditions virtually any standard recipe would work. Or to be more precise, we were determined to find conditions that would work with any soap recipe.

What we found was that most illustrated instructions showed hot-process soap that more closely resembled taffy than the soap mixtures we enjoy processing. Yes, taffy. If you ever made any variety of taffy as a child, you will remember buttering your hands as you pull and work this hot, sticky mass, rolling and shaping until it is ready to harden. Most of the pictures of hot-process soap involve producing either a doughy substance or something that looks like thick lubricating grease. Somehow, we just had to resist the attraction of trying to push something like molten asphalt into the corners of a mold. And yet, we knew it was a possibility.

THE FIRST ATTEMPT

There were two opposing ways to attack hot processing. One was to start out using our normal recipes but substitute a crockpot for the steel pot on the stove and maintain a higher temperature until the soap was ready to mold. The second method was to systematically vary conditions to see what effect it would have on processing and the quality of the finished soap. Bob, of course, being the trained scientist, decided we would wing it and just modify our current procedure. This led to the production of a tracing mixture that separated into a caustic water solution and a thick, chunky soap mass as we poured the mixture into the mold. Well, we never walk away from a problem batch. We waited overnight and in the morning we found a watery layer in the mold with a rather slimy chunk of wet soap in the middle. Okay, sometimes it just does not pay to try and salvage an experiment gone so very wrong. So, despite its pleasant pink color and peppermint aroma, the solid went into the trash and the liquid washed down the drain.

As the soap overcooked, it coagulated into a lumpy pink mass surrounded by thin clear liquid.

Hopes that further cooking would produce a homogenous, usable mixture were dashed.

Hope springs eternal, but this batch remained hopelessly in two phases. Into the trash it went.

Sometimes further cooking just produces lumpy, thick soap.

Thirty minutes after trace, the soap could be transferred (with difficulty) and spread or forced into the mold. It still was too thick to produce a level soap and it was filled with gaps and air pockets ... although it was hard.

Within minutes the soap was firm enough to support a spoon or hold a toothpick upright.

NEVER GIVE UP

We were determined to make our second foray into hot processing a true learning experience. We wanted to push the envelope to see just how far we could push the product before it became virtually impossible to handle. This approach worked quite well, but we have to admit, we were extremely tempted to quit when we knew the soap was ready to pour into the mold. Of course, that would have proved virtually nothing except that one can learn from one's mistakes. And so thin trace came and went. Then thick trace (beautifully creamy and thick) came and went, and the soap in the crock began to form a thick chunky solid in the center and liquefy around the hot walls of the crock. Too thick for a stick blender — hand stirring was in order.

We added some essential oil and some dye dissolved in isopropanol to aid mixing, and attempted to stir them into the pot. The alcohol flashed off and the mixture quickly became an asphalt-like substance (in consistency) that produced swirls of color and heavy fragrance. The swirling-color effect was nice and, if it was the effect that we had intended, we would have been quite happy with the result. Unfortunately, we had envisioned a nice uniform pink peppermint-smelling soap. Please don't get us wrong, the soap was pink (streaked) and smelled like peppermint, but it wasn't at all uniform throughout.

As we spread the thick soap around the mold, it did not coalesce into a single layer. It looked just like what it was, a thick mass that had been folded together several times with obvious layers, air pockets and gaps. The good news is that the soap itself had a smooth finish and felt like a soft, smooth plastic. Quite nice really, but not something that could be scaled up or down. We could hardly imagine trying to push this material into a small bar mold; it just would not work. If this were the end of the story, there would not be much in the following pages.

Here you can easily see the gaps and air pockets.

However, we merely repeated our trials, stopping at points where it was obviously ready to mold. That stage was really unmistakable. This is not to say we didn't have more surprises in store for us; but after this experiment — there were no more disasters.

THE BOTTOM LINE

What did we learn from these attempts and our subsequent trials? There are some really good reasons to go hot process, just as there are some drawbacks that you must consider.

ADVANTAGES OF HOT PROCESS

- The most obvious benefit is time savings.
- You can put your oils into a crockpot and turn it on low heat (or set the temperature to around 180 F [82 C] if you have a digital temperature control). This will melt your oils and keep them ready to go whenever you are ready to make your soap.
- You can premix the lye solution when you weigh out your oils and allow it to cool to room temperature before use.
- Once you start, you can get to thick trace in 20 minutes or less, depending on how much and how often you use your stick blender. We have pushed the entire process to roughly 10 minutes from lye addition to pouring the mixture into the mold.
- You can use large or small molds with or without insulation.
- Molds can be left on the counter or placed in the oven. The process is very flexible and the product, usually, is predictable and uniform.

POTENTIAL CONCERNS

- If your lye solution is too hot or your oils hotter than 212 F (100 C) you could vaporize the lye water as you add it, *generating caustic foam* that could steam up into your face.
- You will be *handling very hot ceramic* if you use a crockpot. Add a slippery soap mixture and you easily can break or spill the container and its contents.
- The *soap is hot enough to burn*. It will cling to your skin or clothing and it contains more than a little unreacted, very hot lye.
- The *soap does not quickly rinse off your skin*, so you need to wear gloves and sleeves (apron, long sleeve shirts or similar) for protection.
- *Eye protection* is especially important.
- *Loss of fragrance components*. Your fragrance goes into a hot, very alkaline mixture. This can lead to evaporative losses

as well as degradation of sensitive fragrance components such as aldehydes. This could be a problem with citrus types of fragrances, which contain citral in addition to more stable components such as limonene. It's difficult to gauge fragrance levels. Hot soap is redolent from your fragrance material (think magnification of scent by about a factor of 10).

- Once the soap cools and hardens, *what fragrance level will you have?* It is hard to tell on the fly; you have to know in advance what you are going to use. Many essential oils can be added at the rate of 10ml (2 teaspoons) per 1kg (2.2 pounds) of oil to give a moderate fragrance level. Fragrance oils usually require at least 50 percent more, but there is no absolute rule. Experience is the best teacher.

- *Over thickening.* Ideally, you will pour a mixture very reminiscent of yogurt into the mold. However, if you wait too long, it will get so thick that it will not pour and you will be trying to "spread" the soap mixture into your molds.

- Our experience shows that when using a stick blender in a crockpot, it is very easy to tilt and cause *splashing of hot soap mixture out of the pot.* Even when using the lid of the pot as a splash guard, it's easy for the mixture to splash out of the container.

- It is a matter of shape and volume. The stick blender causes a rise in the liquid level, which often escapes, even when very thick. This is *messy and potentially dangerous.* If the hot liquid rises above the lip or if it sprays, it can burn either thermally or chemically and/or spray all over any exposed surface.

- Potential *difficulties in scaling up.* A crockpot full of yogurt-like soap mixture is one thing. Forty or 60 liters (10 or 15 gallons) in a Hobart mixer can be exceptionally challenging to transfer into a mold. For that matter, scaling up the mixing with a stick blender virtually is impossible unless you use an extruder. For balance, it is not completely necessary to scale up mixing since through-

put (amount of product made per hour) is usually the key in large-scale reactions, and that is easy to achieve.

- *Issues with FD&C dye colors.* Since you must mix in your colors when the soap mixture is hot and thick, you will need to premix the dyes to make a color concentrate. While you can add dyes as solids to CP soap, this causes problems in HP mixtures. Specifically, the color does not appear (at all) until the temperature and lye concentration both fall to lower levels. It is very difficult to determine exactly what is the most important factor, but rapid chilling (like what happens in a small mold) of the HP with dye will cause it to set up without developing any appreciable color. Without color, it's challenging to determine the appropriate color level for the product.

- *Miscellaneous difficulties.* It is difficult, but not impossible, to make smaller batches other than using one kilogram of oils. However, the walls of the container must be high if you use a stick blender. We have used a one-liter (about one quart) glass container with very high walls to process soap from as little as 350 to 400 grams (12 to 14 ounces) of oil. At some point, it just is not feasible to use a stick blender — you will have to substitute a whisk or some alternate type of mixer.

DO THE BENEFITS OUTWEIGH THE RISKS?

We cannot answer for everyone, but for us, as small-scale soap makers producing designer batches of 3.8L to 11.4L (1 to 3 gallons) at a time, the answer is a resounding *YES.* No, they don't make 7.6L (2-gallon) crockpots, but stove-top reactions can be controlled and there is sufficient latitude in conditions to adapt for virtually all recipes and small-scale volumes in the order mentioned.

Crockpot Soap 1

INS: 120
Lye discount as written: 5 percent

INGREDIENTS

200 grams (7.05 ounces) coconut oil
400 grams (12.60 ounces) shortening
400 grams (14.10 ounces) canola oil
135 grams (4.74 ounces) lye dissolved in 270 grams (9.52 ounces) of distilled water (room temperature)
2.5 to 5 milliliters (0.5 to 1 teaspoon) pigment-type colorant
5 to 8 milliliters (1 to 1.5 teaspoons) bergamot essential oil
Recommended molds: 20 cm x 20 cm (8" x 8") silicone pan, loaf or muffin molds (can be found at low-cost department stores or discount superstores).

PROCEDURE

1. Weigh the oils and transfer to a crockpot. We used a 2.9L (3-quart) crock for the development work but a larger crock is really needed when using a stick blender. Cover the pot.

2. Turn the crockpot to "keep warm" unless you can closely watch the temperatures. Periodically check on the temperature until it reaches between 175 F to 185 F (80 C to 85 C).

Here the oils are heating in the crockpot, ready to go.

3. Add the lye solution slowly at first with gentle stirring. The lye can be added over a period of 30 to 45 seconds or, at this scale, over 1 to 2 minutes. The temperature in the pot will fall to about 130 F to 150 F (55 C to 60 C).

4. Once the lye has been added to the oils, insert the stick blender at the side of the crock, cover the pot as much as possible to prevent serious splashing and start the blender. Be very careful to keep the blender almost upright to avoid splashing contents out of the crock. Pulse the blender on and off over a period of about 30 seconds until the oil/lye has emulsified — a condition similar to a very thin trace.

It is a balancing act. You must avoid splashing caustic liquid out of the crockpot when using the stick blender.

This is soap at thin trace. Notice it still is quite yellow.

This soap has just been poured into the mold. If it is very thick, the surface is difficult to smooth.

5. Remove the blender and cover the crock.

6. Wait approximately 10 minutes and then use the stick blender, pulsing on and off every few seconds until the mixture thickens and achieves full trace, about 60 seconds. (The temperature will climb over the waiting period until it is nearly as high as the initial temperature).

8. Turn off the crockpot. Using potholders or cloths remove the crock and move it to the molding area.

9. Carefully grasp the crock and tilt it over the mold to pour the soap mixture. Use a silicone spatula to scrape down the sides of the crock to complete the transfer.

At thick trace with the consistency of pudding, the color has appreciably lightened.

It takes some practice to get the surface smooth (if you don't like the rustic look).

7. Add color and fragrance to the mixture and blend in using the stick blender. You may have to stir around the sidewalls of the crock by hand if the color does not evenly disperse. The stick blender really is not designed to mix in thickened material stuck along the walls of a pot. At this point, the soap is thickening rapidly and should be transferred to the mold without undue delay. The fragrance will be prominent if not intense. The thickness of the soap will be quite like spoonable pudding.

10. Smooth the surface of the soap as needed. If you look at the soap after another 30 to 60 minutes, you will see the center turning almost translucent as a gel forms. The gel will solidify and become opaque as the soap cools further.

Chapter Ten: Hot-Process Soap Making

Approximately 10 to 15 minutes after pouring, you can see the gel phase begin to set in.

This is about the maximum gel visible. Notice that the cooler edges solidify but do not gel. This creates a different appearance along the edges but all of it is good soap.

Here the surface is relatively solid but the gel phase is visible through cracks in the surface. These cracks can be mostly avoided by allowing the soap/mold to set up on a wire rack. It still gels, but rarely creates fissures.

11. Allow the soap to stand 24 to 48 hours then peel the mold from the soap, which is solid, but soft.

12. Allow the soap to stand in air for at least an additional 24 hours and then cut into desired size.

13. Let soap stand an additional 1 to 2 weeks to harden. (The water evaporates leaving behind a harder bar of soap.)

Crockpot Soap II

INS: 145
Lye discount as written: 6.2 percent

INGREDIENTS

300 grams (10.58 ounces) palm kernel oil

400 grams (14.10 ounces) palm oil

300 grams (10.58 ounces) olive oil

135 grams (4.74 ounces) lye dissolved in 270 grams (9.53 ounces) of distilled water (room temperature)

2.5 to 5 milliliters (0.5 to 1 teaspoon) pigment-type colorant

5 to 8 milliliters (1 to 1.5 teaspoons) bergamot essential oil

Crockpot Soap III

INS: 141
Lye discount as written: 6.2 percent

INGREDIENTS

300 grams (10.58 ounces) palm kernel oil

400 grams (14.10 ounces) palm oil

200 grams (7.05 ounces) olive oil

100 grams (3.53 ounces) grape seed oil

135 grams (4.74 ounces) lye dissolved in 270 grams (9.53 ounces) of distilled water (room temperature)

2.5 to 5 milliliters (0.5 to 1 teaspoon) pigment-type colorant

5 to 8 milliliters (1 to 1.5 teaspoons) bergamot essential oil

Crockpot Soap IV

INS: 149
Lye discount as written: 5.8 percent

INGREDIENTS

150 grams (5.29 ounces) shea butter

300 grams (10.58 ounces) olive oil

300 grams (10.58 ounces) shortening

250 grams (8.81 ounces) coconut oil

140 grams (4.92 ounces) lye dissolved in 280 grams (9.88 ounces) of distilled water (room temperature)

2.5 to 5 milliliters (0.5 to 1 teaspoon) pigment-type colorant

5 to 8 milliliters (1 to 1.5 teaspoons) bergamot essential oil

Crockpot Soap V

INS: 144
Lye discount as written: 3.5 percent

INGREDIENTS

300 grams (10.58 ounces) shortening

50 grams (1.76 ounces) jojoba oil

150 grams (5.29 ounces) shea butter

250 grams (8.81 ounces) olive oil

250 grams (8.81 ounces) coconut oil

140 grams (4.92 ounces) lye dissolved in 280 grams (9.88 ounces) of distilled water (room temperature)

2.5 to 5 milliliters (0.5 to 1 teaspoon) pigment-type colorant

5 to 8 milliliters (1 to 1.5 teaspoons) bergamot essential oil

Crockpot Soap VI

INGREDIENTS

INS: 135
Lye discount as written: 5 percent

200 grams (7.05 ounces) coconut oil
50 grams (1.76 ounces) cocoa butter
50 grams (1.76 ounces) jojoba oil
100 grams (3.53 ounces) castor oil
200 grams (7.05 ounces) canola oil
300 grams (10.58 ounces) palm oil
100 grams (3.53 ounces) olive oil
135 grams (4.74 ounces) lye dissolved in 270 grams (9.53 ounces) of distilled water (room temperature)
2.5 to 5 milliliters (0.5 to 1 teaspoon) pigment-type colorant
5 to 8 milliliters (1 to 1.5 teaspoons) bergamot essential oil

HOT-PROCESS SOAP MAKING WITH OVEN FINISH

It was while we were experimenting with hot process that we made a key discovery about reaction times. We actually were trying to film a video on the entire process and had achieved a nice thin trace when Bob reached for a D&C dye to use as a colorant. As the "film was rolling" Bob added a small scoop of dye and, when the color did not change appreciably, he added another. Since time was limited we just kept on going and kept our disappointment over the lack of color to ourselves. Soon the soap had thickened, the camera stopped, we poured the soap into its mold, cleaned up the workspace and left.

The next day Bob went to check on the soap and was quite startled to find a rather intense blue soap staring back at him. There were, in fact, small dots of more intense color speckled about the soap. This set us back in our tracks and we questioned whether the dyes could be reliably used in hot-process soap. What had happened? This accidental result put a temporary halt to our investigative work, at least with using dyes — pigment colorants were unaffected as you might expect.

Speckled blue that developed using (too much) dye colorant.

After sleeping on this unexpected result for a week, we came up with a way to determine what had happened. Bob remembered that his chemistry students had achieved some unexpected results when using a mixed pH indicator with strong bases. The color they achieved was not even listed on the indicator bottle, though at moderate pH, the expected colors were clearly observed.

The defining experiment had two parts, a small control and the larger experimental part of the batch. We selected a nice green dye and juniper berry essential oil for the scent. We used our standard oil blend to avoid introducing a new set of variables, and started out to make a batch of hot-process soap where the thickened soap was kept at an elevated temperature in the oven. When the batch had achieved trace, the colorant and fragrance were added, though no color change was observed. The bulk of the mixture was put into a square silicone mold while a smaller portion was scraped into a shallow 5cm by 5cm (2" by 2") mold. The small mold was kept at room temperature and the larger silicone mold was rushed into the oven … we anxiously waited.

After about an hour, the oven sample was gelling as expected, but no color change was observed in either sample. After two hours, we turned the oven off and allowed the temperature to slowly drift downward. In four hours the oven temperature had drifted to about 113 F (45 C) and the soap in the oven finally turned a satisfying pale green. The smaller room-temperature sample still had not developed color. After some five hours, we removed the (green) oven sample and allowed it to stand alongside the unchanged room-temperature sample.

At that point, we thought we understood what was happening, but our theory required that the smaller sample turn green overnight or over some extended period of time. And, yes, indeed, the next day the small sample had finally changed color to match the larger sample. What does this suggest? At high pH, very alkaline conditions, the dyes are colorless. As the lye is consumed making soap by saponification, the pH drops. Eventually, the pH drops to a point where the dye molecule undergoes the expected change and produces color. In the case of hot-process soap finished in the oven, saponification is substantially completed over the first four hours. In the case of the smaller sample that cools quickly, the same degree of saponification requires much more time, and that same point was reached at some time during the next 12 to 16 hours.

We knew all of this instinctively, but here was some actual proof that hot-process soap gets milder sooner. In fact, the hotter the soap is kept, the sooner the total and complex reactions are completed. If you had the oven space, you actually could keep the soap hot enough to dehydrate it (to make it harder and resist softening during use) and be usable almost at once. Here, at last, was our proof.

PROCEDURE

1. Preheat oven to 170 F (77 C).

2. Use any HP recipe and proceed as for "regular" crockpot hot-process soap (i.e. follow steps 1 through 6 on pages 81 to 82).

3. As soon as your soap has been poured into the mold, transfer it to the oven. Allow it to rest for at least one hour and then turn off the oven, but allow the soap to remain in the oven for an additional 3 to 4 hours.

This soap, kept out of the oven, is still white after four hours.

During the same time, the soap kept warm in the oven developed its color and turned green.

4. Remove the soap and allow it to stand at room temperature for 24 to 48 hours.

5. Un-mold and, after an additional 24 hours, cut into appropriate-size bars.

6. Store the bars in the open air for an additional 1 to 2 weeks to allow the soap to harden as desired.

Silicone molds designed for cupcakes, including heart shapes, can be found in kitchen stores.

Peel off the mold from the soap; it is ready to cut into desired shapes.

These were made in individual molds designed to produce embossing.

You can cut soap with a clay wire cutter. Pull the wire down through the soap.

You also can use a firm knife with an even thin blade to cut the blocks into bars.

The appropriate dimensions are marked as cutting begins.

Chapter Ten: Hot-Process Soap Making

— Chapter Eleven —
BISON SOAP MAKING

Until recently, bison evoked either an image of the Old West or some guy at a farmers market selling specialty meat products. Then, we received an email from someone who wanted to know the SAP for bison soap making. We immediately went searching through our books and on the Internet to locate the desired information. Unfortunately, we didn't find it, so we went to the source — bison ranchers with commercial meat outlets.

Cut bison soap.

LINDNER BISON™ HERITAGE RANCH

We ultimately discovered the information in a book that was available online, but we also discovered Lindner Bison Heritage Ranch. This family-run business raises 100-percent grass-fed bison in Northern California and sells their meat on the Internet and at farmers markets in Southern California. In fact, we probably walked past the Lindners many times at the Sunday farmers market at the marina in Long Beach. Our inquiries led to an exchange of emails about bison fat (or tallow) soap and to an agreement that we would produce soap for them to sell.

BISON TALLOW (FAT)

Grass-fed bison, exclusively, yield a very hard fat that is yellow in color due to the vitamin E and carotene (a vitamin A precursor), which builds up naturally in the fat of grass-fed animals. This really piqued our interest since our experience has shown the need to incorporate antioxidants into any soap that needs a shelf life of more than one or two months. Although soap does not go bad or turn rancid, oxidation (caused by oxygen in the air) of the fatty acids eventually leads to discoloration (DOS, or dreaded orange spots) unless you can package the soap in an airtight bag or container. This is not a simple task unless you vacuum-seal it in plastic. On the other hand, vitamin E is an antioxidant we have used for years to improve the stability of soap that is stored in the open. Using bison tallow as a soap base sounded like a win-win situation.

Raw bison fat.

Bison fat goes into crockpot.

We had some trepidation (caused by more than a dozen years in the industry making industrial surfactants from beef tallow and yellow grease) about our first bison soap trials. Fortunately, the Lindners provided us with finely ground (much easier to handle) hard kidney fat; unrefined fat requires an extra step — rendering.

Previously, we limited our use of fats to commercially processed shortening or food-grade lard, which doesn't require any additional processing steps. Thankfully, our concern was needless. Soon we discovered that the rendering process was very simple and resulted in a hard, yellowish and virtually odorless fat, which was ready to use for conversion to soap. We might add that the soap we prepared set up fast, had a very smooth surface despite bulging ominously as it passed through the gel stage, and quickly produced a very hard bar of soap. So if you're looking for a natural, sustainable, antioxidant-rich, hard feedstock, find the bison supplier nearest you and try making soap from bison fat.

Filtering out cracklings.

Residue from rendering.

Chapter Eleven: Bison Soap Making

RENDERING: OVEN METHOD

Pre-heat the oven between 250 F and 275 F (121 C to 135 C). Place roughly 900 grams (2 pounds) of bison fat in an uncovered stainless steel pot and place in the oven. It will take approximately one hour to melt the fat and reach the point where solid "cracklings" are visible in the pot.

Don't worry; the solids are natural and easily removed by straining the melted fat through a splatter-guard screen. Do not squeeze or press the cracklings to avoid pushing more protein into the fat. Although sieves can be used, the extra thickness in sieves makes it very difficult to thoroughly clean between batches. A "loose mesh" splatter guard is a better choice to filter out the solids.

Strain the fat into a square silicone cake pan and allow fat to harden into a nice yellow solid weighing roughly 750 grams (26.5 ounces). This is an 83 percent yield of usable bison tallow.

RENDERING: CROCKPOT METHOD

Place 2.26 kilograms (5 pounds) of bison tallow into a crockpot. Set the pot on low heat and stir the fat every 30 minutes until all the fat has melted (will take roughly 2 to 2.5 hours). Using a ladle, transfer the fat to a silicone cake pan, filtering through a splatter guard to remove solids. After cooling (about 2 hours) the solidified fat will be ready to use without further processing. However, if the fat is not to be used right away, it must be transferred into a plastic bag and stored in the refrigerator or freezer until needed.

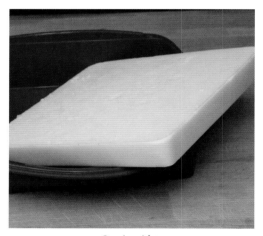

Rendered fat.

Melting fat and oils.

Bison soap entering gel stage.

BISON SOAP

The color of this natural soap is a very pale yellow (almost white) and nearly odorless. It is a very attractive bar. Any fatty odor usually disappears within days as the soap dries.

Bison Soap Recipe I

INGREDIENTS

150 grams (5.3 ounces) canola oil
225 grams (8 ounces) palm kernel oil
650 grams (23 ounces) bison fat, rendered
142 grams (5.02 ounces) lye
285 grams (10.1 ounces) distilled water
1.2 milliliters (0.25 teaspoon) ROE or your choice

INS: 166
Lye discount as written: 3.5 percent
Contains 22 percent palm kernel oil

Optional: Color of choice

PROCEDURE

1. Using recipe No. 1 or No. 2, melt oils together in a pan or crockpot set to low heat. Due to the high melting point of bison fat, the final temperature will be around 180 F to 185 F (83 C to 85 C).

2. Dissolve 142 grams of lye in 285 grams of distilled water. Allow to cool slightly before using.

3. Remove the melted oil from the heat and slowly add the lye solution to the oil while pulsing with your stick blender.

4. When the mixture thickens to trace (this mixture thickens quickly) add the fragrance and color of your choice.

5. Transfer to a silicone or flexible plastic mold using a spatula to scrape down the sides of the pot.

6. In approximately 30 minutes, you may see the soap start to bulge up as it enters the gel stage. However, the finished soap should have a flat surface. This recipe was a bit unusual in that we observed the soap gelling in individual molds, though this rarely happens due to the higher surface-to-volume ratio of small molds.

7. After 24 hours, carefully remove the soap from the mold by flexing and peeling the mold away from the soap. If you plan to cut the soap into smaller pieces, this should be done within 24 hours of unmolding due to the hardness of the soap. Aged any longer, the soap will be so hard that it will be difficult to cut and produce a soap bar with a clean, sharp edge.

8. The yield of soap before curing was roughly 1.27kg (2.8 pounds).

Bison Soap Recipe II

INGREDIENTS

500 grams (17.7 ounces) canola oil
375 grams (13.3 ounces) coconut oil
875 grams (30.9 ounces) bison fat, rendered
245 grams (8 ounces) lye dissolved in 490 grams (16 ounces) distilled water

INS: 156
Lye discount as written: 5 percent
Contains 21.4 percent palm kernel oil

This is a larger recipe, suitable for making in a crockpot.

— Chapter Twelve —

SIMPLE LIQUID PRODUCTS — GREEN AND NATURAL

Green is the thing. Natural is the thing. Energy efficiency and environmentally friendly ingredients are important and growing segments in nearly every market. But there definitely are different perspectives about what qualifies as green and natural. Green ordinarily means environmentally friendly. However, this can encompass materials made from renewable resources, materials with minimal processing (minimizes waste and energy consumption), biodegradable, low toxicity and safe to use.

THE GREEN MARKET

The authority on the market for green and natural products appears to be the Lifestyles of Health and Sustainability (LOHAS) study. According to this and related studies, there are three major segments of the population that are concerned with green products. These segments of adult U.S. consumers account for approximately 63 percent of adults.

The first group, termed LOHAS consumers, represent the core target market for all things healthy and sustainable. These are identified as highly motivated consumers who lead the way in adopting "green" or natural products. They specifically seek out and live a "healthy lifestyle." Nineteen percent of the U.S. adult population is identified in this category (some 41 million adults out of an estimated population of 125 million). The total market for this segment is approximately $109 billion for natural/organic personal health care products.

So-called "Naturalites" are a secondary target for natural or organic products in personal care. These consumers are interested in personal health, but choose a less driven approach to incorporating natural and organic products into their purchasing decisions. For these consumers, the natural/organic label is a preference, not a must. These "light green" consumers constitute another 19 percent of the adult market.

The last key segment is sometimes identified as "Drifters." These are younger consumers who often are under the direct influence of their parents. These are wannabes who do not or cannot make an overt decision to purchase this type of product. It could be cost driven, as many "Drifters" are not fully established and financially independent. Some, of course, may still reside with their parents and not participate fully and independently in the full spectrum of purchasing decisions. It is important to reach these consumers, which comprise approximately 25 percent of the adult market — they are the future or potential of the market.

GREEN PRODUCTS

Ultimately, there has to be some definition that identifies a product as being made with "green" components and thus should be considered a green product. Obviously, a green surfactant base must come from vegetable products rather than petroleum. Minimal processing usually indicates that the base is either a fatty acid or a fatty alcohol, which essentially is one process removed from the fatty acid. The difficulty, then, is how to finish the surfactant in order to achieve functionality, which must provide a balance between mildness, foaming, cleaning and viscosity.

"GREEN" INGREDIENTS

Potential natural chemicals that might be used to provide different functionality include sugars such as glucose, glycerin, sorbitol; and short diacids such as succinic acid, which can either be derived from natural organic sources or produced from petroleum products. Petroleum occurs naturally (in the earth from whence it is pumped). Less desirable, from a green perspective, is ethylene oxide, which is derived from petroleum or natural gas. Amines, especially when two or three ethanol groups are attached, often are used with fatty acids to produce salts or condensed amides. The ethanol usually comes from ethylene oxide, so that detracts from the overall acceptability. In fact, relative "greenness" often is judged by the relative number of carbons from natural sources versus the total number of carbons in the surfactant.

More problematic is sulfation or sulfonation, the addition of the components of sulfuric acid. This is an inorganic material, which can lead to harsh products, toxic byproducts and difficult waste streams. Used properly, sulfate derivatives add tremendous functionality. Sulfate derivatives are highly water-soluble and help make solutions or emulsions between materials that are otherwise incompatible. In the end, green surfactants must tread a fine line to produce a product that can be successfully blended into a variety of useful products.

SELLING AND LABELING YOUR GREEN PRODUCT

Let us add here a word of caution. All water-soluble surfactants should be considered *eye and skin irritants* if used in high concentration or left on the skin for long periods of time. Surfactants generally are designed to dissolve fats. Cell membranes are lipids, a class of fatty materials. This leads to irritation and potential damage through contact. Before you sell any formulated liquid product, you need to look into the regulations that govern the product and its contents. Most of these regulations can be found online in the Code of Federal Regulations (CFR). Labeling requirements are either detailed by the CFR or the general requirements of the Federal Trade Commission (FTC). Most liquid products fall under the regulations of one or both of these federal agencies and, in addition to labeling issues, require adherence to good manufacturing procedures and record keeping. The requirements often are so detailed and so specific to one type of product (e.g. shampoo, bubble bath, skin cleanser) that they are impossible to summarize in a short space.

There just isn't enough time or space in one chapter to fully describe the wide range of surfactants available for formulating green products, so we'll focus on some of our favorite materials. We will explain what they do, describe how they relate to green and provide you with a formulation or two where they are used to impart functionality. It is a great starting point if you want to add liquid products to your line.

SURFACTANTS

Oleic Acid Diethanolamide. This product starts with oleic acid, a natural fatty acid found in high amounts in olive and canola oils as well as in animal fat. Dehydration synthesis (condensation reaction) between oleic acid and diethanolamine produces the diethanolamide plus water. This is a nonionic surfactant with good water solubility due to the two hydroxyethyl groups attached to the amide nitrogen. As with all surfactants, it is an eye irritant and considered a mild skin irritant as well (in high concentrations). This type of amide generally is used to simultaneously thicken a formulation and stabilize foam. Eighteen out of its total 22 carbons are derived from natural, renewable resources. Pilot Chemical Company sells this type of product as Calamide®F, a 46 percent aqueous solution.

Fatty Acid Amide Ethoxylates. These materials are produced by the dehydration synthesis (condensation) reaction of a fatty acid with a polyethoxylated primary amine, forming an ethoxylated amide plus water. These surfactants tend to be mild; although, because they often are supplied at a pH of 9 to 11, the solutions available are alkaline and thus irritating to eyes and skin. All ethoxylates have the potential to contain the byproduct dioxane and may fall under the SARA Title III (Superfund Amendments Reauthorization Act) and various state regulations (e.g. California Proposition 65), even though the product itself may not belong to any regulated (hazardous) transportation classification.

Oleamide DEA or Oleic Acid Diethanolamide.

Disodium Lauryl Sulfosuccinate.

One commercially available product, a high-solids liquid (>90 percent solids) from Kao Chemicals Europe, is derived from rapeseed fatty acid (16 to 18 carbon chainlength) and triethyleneglycolamine. Kao reports uses as a mild thickener, foam booster and co-surfactant, imparting a pleasant skin feel to formulations. It has on average 17 out of a total of 23 carbons derived from natural, renewable resources.

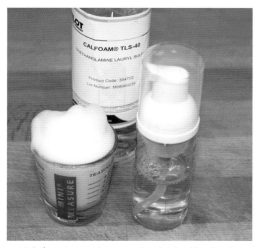

High-foaming products can be obtained by diluting commercial blended concentrates.

TEA-Lauryl Sulfate and Sodium Lauryl Sulfate (SLS). Both of these begin with coconut oil, which is high in lauric acid (a 12-carbon fatty acid). The oil is hydrogenated to the fatty alcohol, which is further reacted with sulfuric acid and neutralized. The use of sodium carbonate in the neutralization step produces SLS while neutralization with triethanolamine produces the milder TEA-Lauryl Sulfate. These both are highly functional surfactants, which produce high foam or lather. SLS also is very inexpensive, which leads to its use in many products, especially toothpaste. The efficiency of SLS gives it the ability, in high concentrations, to dissolve cell membranes causing cell destruction on the micro scale and skin irritation on the macro scale. For this reason, we cannot recommend the use of SLS in bubble bath-type formulations despite its ability to produce high levels of bubbles. The TEA salt is less irritating in skin contact and often is used in cosmetic formulations. Both substances are used to enhance foaming or lather in formulations. The TEA salt has 12 of 18 total carbons derived from natural, renewable products. Pilot

Chemical Company sells Calfoam®TLS-40, a 40 percent aqueous solution of the TEA salt.

Sodium Lauryl Ether Sulfate (SLES or SLAES). Another way to somewhat lessen the irritation of alcohol sulfates is to sulfate an ethoxylated alcohol. In this case, the coconut derived lauryl alchol is first reacted with two to three moles of ethylene oxide followed by reaction with sulfuric acid. All ethoxylates have the potential to contain the byproduct dioxane and may fall under the SARA Title III (Superfund Amendments Reauthorization Act) and various state regulations (e.g. California Proposition 65) even though the product itself may not belong to any regulated (hazardous) transportation classification. SLAES is considered to be readily biodegradable. SLAES is available from Pilot Chemical Company as Calfoam®ES-302, a 27 percent aqueous solution of the two-mole ethoxylate. As the name suggests, it is used as a foam booster in formulations. This SLAES has 12 out of 16 carbons derived from natural, renewable resources.

Sodium Lauryl Sulfoacetate (SLSA). Condensing lauryl alcohol with sulfoacetic acid makes this mild surfactant. Although the name sounds very similar to sodium lauryl sulfate, the sulfur is attached directly to carbon, not as an ester through a sulfate oxygen. This alters the chemistry and makes a much milder surfactant, which still has high foaming ability. It is often found pre-blended in surfactant, ready to use formulations such as Stepan-Mild LSB available from the Stepan Company (Northfield, Illinois). It also can be purchased as a pure solid from other soap supply companies, such as Majestic Mountain Sage (see suppliers on pages 149 to 150. SLSA has 12 out of 14 total carbons derived from natural, renewable resources.

Disodium Lauryl Sulfosuccinate. This mild, high-foaming surfactant is produced from lauryl alcohol (from coconut oil) by first reacting it with maleic acid to form the lauryl maleate ester. This ester is then further reacted with sodium sulfite, which adds across the maleic acid double bond to form the sulfosuccinate. Another common sulfosuccinate is the disodium laureth sulfosuccinate, which typically uses a three-mole ethoxylated lauryl alcohol to react with maleic acid. Lauryl sulfosuccinate has 12 out of 16 carbons from natural, renewable

Lauryl Sulfoacetate.

One form of Cocoamidopropylbetaine.

resources while the ethoxylated version has only 12 out of 22 carbons from natural, renewable resources.

Cocoamidopropyl Betaine (CAPB). Betaines are zwitterionic substances, meaning the compounds contain both positive- and negative-charged centers. CAPB can be regarded as a composition of two natural materials, coconut fatty acid and glycine betaine. However, it ordinarily is produced by a two-step synthesis where coconut fatty acids are first reacted with dimethylaminopropylamine to produce an amino amide followed by reaction with sodium chloroacetate to produce the final CAPB. Due to the mild nature of this material, betaines are used in shampoos, hand soaps and cosmetics, often replacing much harsher ingredients in whole or part. It still must be considered an eye irritant as well as a mild skin irritant, especially in high concentrations. It thickens and has some antistatic activity in hair conditioners, and is reported to have antiseptic properties. It is compatible with cationic, anionic and nonionic surfactants. Due to the synthetic production of one of the starting materials, it can only be considered to have 12 or 13 carbons out of 17 or 18 total carbons that are derived from natural, renewable resources. It can be purchased pre-blended with other surfactants or as a 30-percent aqueous solution as Caltaine C-35 from Pilot Chemical Company.

QUANTITY DECISIONS

Here comes the tricky part. You now have a list of surfactants as well as an idea about how they stack up as natural and renewable or green materials. This should enable you to evaluate many of the liquid products you have in your own home. Look at the label. If it claims to be a green product, how do the ingredients back up that statement?

If you want to formulate your own liquid products, you have a number of choices to make. How expensive can the product be to make? If you are making your own, this largely is a matter of the cost of raw materials. How many ingredients can you stock? How many ingredients can you get in reasonable quantities to fit your scale of operation? If you are a large-scale operation, you probably can purchase in drum quantities. If you are looking for five-gallon quantities, you may have to go to a distributor who adds his cost on top of the manufacturer's cost. If you are looking to make, over the course of a year, a hundred bottles of liquid product, then you will have to use smaller quantities and you may find that it is unrealistically expensive to stock three to five separate ingredients for blending.

The answer for most small businesses is the use of pre-blended mixtures, available through most manufacturers. These blends can be diluted, pH adjusted, colored, scented and thickened in order to produce your own unique product. Even better, assuredly, the manufacturer will have a technical service department to offer you formulations they have developed over time, which may well meet your needs.

Remember, as you dilute the blends, the viscosity generally will decrease as well, though some blends may surprise you. Thickening often can be achieved by the addition of a few percent of sodium chloride or, at a pH of six or below, ammonium chloride. (At a pH above seven, ammonium chloride will free up ammonia, which will dominate any scent you use.)

BLENDS READILY AVAILABLE
FOR YOU TO FOLLOW

Calblend Clear, Pilot Chemical Company: This is one of several blended products that Pilot offers as materials designed to be diluted to the desired concentration, colored and scented. Calblend Clear is a blend of sodium laureth sulfate, cocoamidopropyl betaine, and cocamide DEA with a total water content of roughly 65 percent (or total solids, about 35 percent).

Calblend Eco-1, Pilot Chemical Company: Pilot stresses that this material is made from vegetable sources and is both economical and environmentally friendly (and biodegradable). It is a blend of sodium laureth sulfate, sodium lauryl sulfate, cocamidopropyl betaine and cocamide monoethanolamine (Cocamide MEA).

Stepan-Mild LSB, Stepan Company: This is a blend of disodium laureth sulfosuccinate and lauryl sulfoacetate. It contains roughly 75 percent water, which leaves 20 to 25 percent total surfactants in the package.

— Chapter Thirteen —
SOAP RECIPES

Once you try a few basic recipes and gain confidence in making soap, you probably will want to spread your wings and try other oils, additives and combinations. These recipes use the temperatures and conditions given in previous chapters. Most of the combinations given here contain three or more oils in order to provide a balance of properties (hardness, lather, mildness) in the finished soap.

COLOR AND FRAGRANCES

In general, the colors and fragrances used in soap are not a requirement of the basic recipe. Fragrances are discussed in detail in Chapter 6, although we have made a few suggestions for the optional addition of some essential oils. Remember that herbs, fragrances, colorants and preservatives are all added "at trace" (when the batch thickens to the point where the soap stays in suspension and any residual oil and water [lye solution] no longer separates into layers).

OUR RECIPES

Our own soap recipes are based on blends of olive, coconut, soy or canola and palm oils. As we developed these recipes, we wrote a computer spreadsheet to help us calculate the fatty-acid distribution available from a blend of oils. We knew that we needed to have at least 15 percent by weight of coconut oil for good sudsing, but over 50 percent could result in a harsh soap. Trial and error with oil content and reaction conditions (we meant to say a carefully designed experimental plan followed by in-depth statistical analysis of the results) gave us soap that exceeded

KNOW YOUR MARKET

Although we have dedicated Chapter 11 to making bison soap, most of our recipes do not use tallow or lard (beef and pork fat respectively) for several reasons:

1. Animal fats are objectionable to some people for a variety of health, ethical or religious reasons. Since we sell our soap, we do not want to alienate any potential consumers.

2. The odor of animal fats is not as bland as the odor of vegetable oils, which makes scenting more difficult.

3. Although lard is available in most grocery stores, tallow must either be rendered from butcher's scraps or purchased from a meat packer or broker (i.e. it is hard to get in a directly usable form). On the other hand, if you have access to a local supply of fats, you can substitute lard or tallow for some or all of the palm and soy oils in our recipes, making the appropriate adjustments in the amount of lye required.

our original demands and expectations.

Our recipes are geared to make good soap in reasonable time. We have tried to balance the fatty-acid distribution by means of these blends to have enough lauric acid (from coconut) to provide good lathering; enough long-chain fatty acids from olive and soy for good oily soil removal and mildness; and enough palm oil to provide hardness and density in the finished bar.

Tallow or a mixture of tallow and lard is used in most commercial soaps and can make an outstanding cold-process soap and one that is easily rebatched. Furthermore, a soap made with high lard content is very useful in the laundry, especially to pretreat stubborn soils and stains. If you don't mind the extra work, lard, which is readily available, is an extremely useful tool in your soap design arsenal. See Chapter 11: Bison Soap Making.

For those who do not want to use either tallow or lard and who do not have access to palm oil, consider vegetable shortening, especially if made from cottonseed oil. Due to nutrition concerns, cottonseed oil accounts for only about 3 percent of oils used to make shortening in the U.S. today. However, the fatty-acid distribution of partially hydrogenated cottonseed oil is quite similar to lard and shortenings containing all or mostly partially hydrogenated cottonseed oil and it makes a good substitute. In general, switching between most vegetable shortenings (made mostly from partially hydrogenated soybean oil) and lard will work, but the substitution is not as close a fit. Although we do make some superfatted soap, the bulk of the soap we produce has nearly a 1:1 ratio of fatty acids to lye. People with dry skin can tolerate, even need, extra emollients, while others may break out as a result of the extra oil.

Highly superfatted soaps often will need the addition of antioxidants as they can become rancid (dry soap will resist rancidity since bacterial growth requires moisture) when left in contact with water. The simplest antioxidants are natural oils, which are sources of vitamin A or E. Wheat germ oil and carrot seed oil are suitable natural sources. Grapefruit seed extract is sometimes used with the extra benefit of shortening the overall reaction time for saponification, although one should not totally rely on grapefruit seed extract to avoid rancidity and off colors.

Rosemary oil extract (ROE) also is becoming readily available and has a well-documented history of commercial use in stabilizing oils and oil derivatives. It probably is the most promising antioxidant now on the market. We use ROE with a 5 percent carnosic acid content. This component is widely held to be the most active component in ROE. The ROE will impart a temporary dark brown color that quickly fades away as the soap sets up. ROE arguably is the most used antioxidant in the home/handmade soap market.

You also may find vitamin E or vitamin E oil at your drugstore. Vitamin E oil is simply vitamin E supplied in a vegetable oil carrier; and the carrier oil should be included in your lye calculations.

Vitamin C, ascorbic acid, also is an antioxidant. However, ascorbic acid will consume lye. Approximately 0.23 grams of lye will be neutralized for every gram of ascorbic acid added. Depending on your recipe, you might need to add additional lye to neutralize the added ascorbic acid. Most vitamins are available in natural or synthetic forms. The effectiveness of synthetic forms can vary according to the nature of the synthetic and the desired function.

A FEW THOUGHTS ON YIELD

By this time you probably are starting to wonder, "How many molds do I need?" or "How much soap will the recipe actually make?" The simplistic answer is that it depends on the type of molds you are using. That information, however, is not particularly helpful, especially when you have a pot of soap that is starting to get thick and you are suddenly wondering where you are going to put it all.

Here are a few guiding thoughts about molds and volume. When we make soap, we ordinarily use 74ml to 118ml (2.5 to 4 fluid-ounce) plastic molds. The number of soap bars depends on how many 74ml (2.5-ounce) molds we use compared to how many 118ml (4-ounce) molds, but in general, our recipes that use 680g (24 ounces) of lye (by weight) generally yield about 55 to 60 bars of soap, which weigh a total of approximately 6.8kg (15 pounds). Recipes that call for added solids such as ground oatmeal or pumice make a few more bars than those without. For those of you who choose PVC pipe molds, a 76cm (18-inch) piece of 8cm (3-inch) inner diameter pipe has an inner volume of roughly 2L (70 fluid ounces). This means that it would take two full 46cm (18-inch) sections of pipe mold to contain the recipe we mentioned above. If you have a rectangular plastic container or stainless steel baking pan with dimensions of 25cm by 41cm by 5cm (10-inch by 16-inch by 2-inch), the contained volume is approximately 5L (177 fluid ounces) (not enough volume for this recipe, which can produce up to 7L [240 fluid ounces] of raw soap).

COMMERCIAL SOAP MAKING

Some of you may enter the commercial realm of soap making. That is, you will one day start to sell the soap you make. (You only can use or give away so much soap and soap making is addictive!) For commercial enterprises — weight generally is the important factor — not volume. In this case, you will be concerned about calculating the yield of these recipes in terms of the weight of soap it will produce. If you want to determine how much soap your recipe will make, try the following method. It's based on the theory that the total raw soap produced is simply the sum of the weights of all the ingredients: oils, lye, water, fragrance materials and other additives.

Weigh everything, add it up, and that is what you will get out of the pot and into your mold. Keep in mind the curing process is also a drying process and, as the soap cures and ages, it dries out and slightly shrinks. There is no simple way to predict the cured weight of a 0.5kg (1-pound) chunk of fresh soap. The only volatile materials (which can evaporate and lower the weight of the finished soap) are the water and fragrance oils you add. An extreme estimate of the final yield of soap would be the sum of the ingredients except for the water you added with the lye. (In reality, you will not lose all of this water; half to two-thirds is more typical.) The amount you actually lose will depend on the humidity and temperature where you cure the soap and the length of curing time.

TIP

Most soap supply dealers offer tray molds that can produce nine to 12 85g to 113g (3- to 4-ounce) bars at a time, once they are cut apart.

Basic Four-Oil Soap I

Nothing too fancy here, just a good blend of oils that make good soap. Add your herbs or fragrance oils at trace. We have indicated the ingredient weights in ounces in parentheses.

Remember, these are weights, not volumes.

INGREDIENTS

725 grams (25.57 ounces) coconut oil

150 grams (5.29 ounces) olive oil

650 grams (22.93 ounces) canola oil

775 grams (27.33 ounces) palm oil

342 grams (12 ounces) lye dissolved in 700 grams
   (24.7 ounces) distilled or deionized water

Okay, so basic soap is white and boring. This basic soap was poured into a loofah (which was wrapped tightly with plastic wrap so the soap would not run out before it solidified.) The soap-filled loofah was sliced into sections using a serrated knife.

INS: 145
Lye discount as written: 6.2 percent

Basic Four-Oil Soap II

This recipe is similar to the previous recipe, except for the substitution of soybean oil for canola. Both are low-cost oils that produce a mild soap, although people with soy allergies may want to stick with the canola formula. We have indicated the ingredients weights in ounces in parentheses.

Remember, these are weights, not volumes.

Tinted with turmeric, this soap has an interesting peachy color, which goes well with apricot fragrance.

INGREDIENTS

1500 grams (52.91 ounces) coconut oil

500 grams (17.64 ounces) olive oil

1400 grams (49.38 ounces) soybean oil

1200 grams (42.33 ounces) palm oil

45 milliliters (3 tablespoons) fragrance oil (add more
   if desired)

684 grams (24 ounces) lye dissolved in 1400 grams
   (49.38 ounces) distilled or deionized water

INS: 152
Lye discount as written: 5 percent

Basic Three-Oil Soap I

This premium soap is made with a high olive oil content for mildness, coconut oil for lather and all-vegetable shortening instead of the harder-to-find palm oil for hardness. These probably are the three easiest ingredients to find when starting out and they make an excellent soap. This recipe will produce a very white soap unless you select a dark green olive oil, which will give it a greenish cast. The weights in ounces are indicated in parentheses.

Remember, these are weights, not volumes.

Turmeric gives the basic color while powdered kelp produces the nice green.

INGREDIENTS

750 grams (26.46 ounces) coconut oil

700 grams (26.69 ounces) olive oil

900 grams (31.75 ounces) shortening

342 grams (12 ounces) lye dissolved in

650 grams (22.93 ounces) distilled or deionized water

INS: 159
Lye discount as written: 5.8 percent

Basic Three-Oil Soap II

We know that some would prefer to begin making soap using more cost-effective oil instead of olive oil. This recipe substitutes canola oil for the olive, but in this case, the amount of shortening must be increased to maintain the hardness and texture of the soap. The weights in ounces are indicated in parentheses.

Remember, these are weights, not volumes.

INGREDIENTS

750 grams (26.46 ounces) coconut oil

700 grams (24.69 ounces) canola oil

1000 grams (35.27 ounces) shortening

342 grams (12 ounces) lye dissolved in

650 grams (22.93 ounces) distilled or deionized water

When we made this batch, we tried out some shocking pink color tabs. We added shavings from the tabs and mixed them in until we got the color we desired. The melt-and-pour color base melts nicely in the cold-process soap at trace. Try a strawberry fragrance oil to go with the color.

INS: 142
Lye discount as written: 7 percent

Basic Soap With Beeswax

Beeswax is often added to hand soaps as it provides extra softening action for rough red hands. It also provides the soap maker with an added benefit — promoting thickening during saponification. This is a good additive for beginners afraid their soap won't solidify. The weights in ounces are indicated in parentheses.

Remember, these are weights, not volumes.

INGREDIENTS

50 grams (1.76 ounces) beeswax

350 grams (12.35 ounces) olive oil

1300 grams (45.86 ounces) coconut oil

1400 grams (49.38 ounces) soybean oil

300 grams (10.58 ounces) palm oil

684 grams (24 ounces) lye dissolved in

1400 grams (49.38 ounces) distilled or deionized water

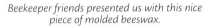

Beekeeper friends presented us with this nice piece of molded beeswax.

INS: 147
Lye discount as written: 7 percent

This soap is colored with cocoa and scented with (artificial) chocolate and vanilla fragrance oils. Although some of the color fades when the soap dries, don't overdo the cocoa. Start with 15ml (1 rounded tablespoon) and check the color.

INS: 150
Lye discount as written: 7 percent

Basic Lard Soap

Some people object to the use of animal products, but animal fat has been used in soap for centuries. In this recipe, the combination of lard and coconut oil help make this a long-lasting bar. The weights in ounces are indicated in parentheses.

Remember, these are weights, not volumes.

INGREDIENTS

928 grams (32.73 ounces) lard

700 grams (24.69 ounces) coconut oil

200 grams (7.05 ounces) olive oil

600 grams (21.16 ounces) canola oil

342 grams (12 ounces) lye dissolved in

700 grams (24.7 ounces) distilled or deionized water

Simple No-Weighing Soap

Okay, so you don't have a scale and can't wait to start making soap. Well, here's a good beginner recipe that calls for oils and other ingredients easy to find in the supermarket and health food store; and everything is measured, not weighed. To add your own personal touch, try adding about 118ml (.05 cup) finely ground oatmeal or 5ml to 10ml (1 to 2 teaspoons) green kelp powder for color. When we made this, we added lily of the valley fragrance oil at light trace, before the soap got too thick. Simple, isn't it?

INGREDIENTS

750 grams (26.46 ounces) coconut oil

700 grams (26.69 ounces) olive oil

900 grams (31.75 ounces) shortening

342 grams (12 ounces) lye dissolved in

650 grams (22.93 ounces) distilled or deionized water

This simple recipe has commonly available ingredients that produce a very nice soap.

Cottonseed Oil Soap With Lanolin

Often soap recipes have been developed at the request of friends. This recipe is in response to a challenge to see what sort of soap could be made using cottonseed oil. We wanted this to be a special hand soap, very moisturizing, so note the use of castor oil for increased lather; lanolin and jojoba oils as emollients; and just a touch of beeswax (mostly used to accelerate saponification). The weights in ounces are indicated in parentheses.

Remember, these are weights, not volumes.

INGREDIENTS

300 grams (10.58 ounces) olive oil

226 grams (7.97 ounces) cottonseed oil

45 grams (1.59 ounces) jojoba oil

320 grams (11.29 ounces) palm oil

625 grams (22.05 ounces) coconut oil

100 grams (3.53 ounces) castor oil

650 grams (22.93 ounces) canola oil

5 grams (0.18 ounce) beeswax

25 grams (0.88 ounce) lanolin

342 grams (12 ounces) lye dissolved in 700 grams (24.7 ounces) distilled or deionized water

Optional: 360 milliliters (0.75 cup) pumice

We planned to make blueberry-scented soap but the blue color tab turned rather beige. We added a hint of violet color tab and left it unscented. It is a nice hand soap made with pumice.

INS: 135
Lye discount as written: 4.2 percent

Tea Tree Oil Bar

A complex blend of vegetable oils, jojoba, aloe vera and tea tree oil make up this special bar soap. Tea tree oil is noted for its antimicrobial, especially antifungal action; it reportedly is absorbed through the skin and can attack subdermal infections. Jojoba and aloe vera nourish the skin. This is a cleansing bar for problem skin areas — fungus, psoriasis, acne — as well as a great bath and shower bar. With its rich creamy lather, it works very well as a shampoo. The tea tree oil and aloe-vera gel are added at trace. The weights in ounces are indicated in parentheses.

Remember, these are weights, not volumes.

INS: 129
Lye discount as written: 10 percent

INGREDIENTS
175 grams (6.17 ounces) olive oil
50 grams (1.76 ounces) jojoba oil
650 grams (22.93 ounces) palm oil
600 grams (21.16 ounces) soy oil
500 grams (17.63 ounces) canola oil
600 grams (21.16 ounces) coconut oil
25 grams (0.88 ounce) tea tree oil
50 grams (1.76 ounces) aloe-vera gel
342 grams (12 ounces) lye dissolved in
    650 grams (22.93 ounces) distilled or
    deionized water

As you can see, pigments provide a nice intense color in a variety of shades. This basically is a white bar, so we added some blue pigment to part of the batch and made white, blue and variegated soap from the same batch.

Oatmeal Facial Bar

Finely ground oatmeal provides gentle abrasion to clear clogged pores and oily skin while jojoba and aloe vera replenish vital nutrients to keep skin clean, healthy and supple. The unique beauty of this golden mottled bar can be enhanced by the addition of a pleasant touch of lavender essential oil. The weights in ounces are indicated in parentheses.

Remember, these are weights, not volumes.

INGREDIENTS
160 grams (5.64 ounces) olive oil
660 grams (23.28 ounces) soy oil
660 grams (23.28 ounces) palm oil
150 grams (5.29 ounces) canola oil
665 grams (23.46 ounces) coconut oil
30 grams (1.06 ounces) jojoba oil
360 milliliters (0.75 cup) ground oatmeal
342 grams (12 ounces) lye dissolved in 700 grams (24.7 ounces) distilled or deionized water
Optional: 12 milliliters (2.5 teaspoons) lavender oil

The actual color of this bar depends on the amount of honey used and the temperature when the honey is added. The color at mixing is fairly dark, but it lightens from a golden to nut brown color as it dries.

INS: 143
Lye discount as written: 3.2 percent

Lavender Goat's Milk Soap

No, this is not made with milk from lavender goats. It is a rich soap containing cocoa butter, jojoba oil, chamomile, powdered goat's milk and lavender essential oil. Chamomile is noted for its healing powers and its rich herbal aroma blends subtly with the lavender. Use an electric food mill to pulverize the chamomile and blend it with the goat's milk solids. These are added, together with the essential oil, at trace; best mixed in with a stainless steel wire whisk. The weights in ounces are indicated in parentheses.

Remember, these are weights, not volumes.

We placed a slice of unscented pale green soap into the mold and then poured goat's milk soap over all to fill the mold.

INGREDIENTS
670 grams (23.64 ounces) canola oil
180 grams (6.35 ounces) olive oil
770 grams (27.16 ounces) palm oil
720 grams (25.40 ounces) coconut oil
20 grams (0.71 ounce) jojoba oil
25 grams (0.88 ounce) cocoa butter
342 grams (12 ounces) lye dissolved in 600 grams (21.2 ounces) distilled or deionized water
50 grams (1.76 ounces) powdered goat's milk
11 grams (0.39 ounce) chamomile, ground
30 milliliters (1 ounce [2 tablespoons]) lavender essential oil

INS: 150
Lye discount as written: 5 percent

Chapter Thirteen: Soap Recipes

Masque de Limone

It is fairly simple to design a good moisturizing soap for dry skin, but we often have been asked for recommendations for oily skin as well. We finally decided to combine several approaches to loosen and remove excess skin oils, replacing them with just a touch of mild jojoba. This lemony bar is the first we have made using the cold process that does not rapidly lose its fresh, lemony scent. Again, an electric food mill is used to pulverize the lemon peel and lemongrass, which are added at trace along with the clay, vitamin E and lemon extract. Be sure to *add the vitamin E before the ground herbs*. The weights in ounces are indicated in parentheses.

Remember, these are weights, not volumes.

This lemon mask has an interesting color all by itself. The aged soap (in hand) is lighter than the freshly made and uncured soap.

INGREDIENTS

303 grams (10.69 ounces) olive oil

1320 grams (46.56 ounces) canola oil

1550 grams (54.67 ounces) palm oil

1460 grams (51.50 ounces) coconut oil

14 grams (.5 ounce) jojoba oil

684 grams (24 ounces) lye dissolved in 1300 grams (45.9 ounces) distilled or deionized water

15 milliliters (0.5 ounce) vitamin E (this can be obtained as virtually 100 percent E but often
  is found diluted in a vegetable oil. You want to use the 100 percent variety here.)

40 grams (1.41 ounces) lemon peel, dried

10 grams (0.35 ounce) ground dried lemongrass

180 milliliters (0.75 cup) French clay

30 milliliters (2 tablespoons) 6x lemon extract
Note: Two tablespoons equal one ounce.

INS: 129 | Lye discount as written: 10 percent

Menthol Mint Shaving Soap

This actually could be called chocolate mint soap, since the cocoa butter brings that lovely chocolate scent through along with the mint. Smells good enough to eat and contains a special blend of ingredients to boost the lather and lubricate and cool the skin. It was designed for a high-altitude army parachutist who needed a very close shave to keep his breathing equipment precisely placed to his face. The weights in ounces are indicated in parentheses.

Remember, these are weights, not volumes.

A little yellow color tab gives a pleasant pale yellow to this minty bar.

INGREDIENTS

50 grams (1.76 ounces) cocoa butter
50 grams (1.76 ounces) shea butter
5 grams (0.18 ounce) beeswax
200 grams (7.05 ounces) castor oil
250 grams (8.82 ounces) olive oil
650 grams (22.93 ounces) coconut oil
400 grams (14.11 ounces) canola oil
670 grams (23.64 ounces) palm oil
50 grams (1.76 ounces) glycerin
342 grams (12 ounces) lye dissolved in 700 grams
    (24.7 ounces) distilled or deionized water

At trace, add:
100 grams (3.53 ounces) clay
20 grams (0.71 ounce) stearic acid
10 grams (0.35 ounce) menthol
5 milliliters (1 teaspoon) camphor
    essential oil

INS: 152
Lye discount as written: 2 percent

Lavender Shampoo/Conditioner Bar

Castor oil is added, together with an additional amount of glycerin, to boost and stabilize the lather. A generous amount of jojoba oil is added to provide conditioning from the fatty alcohol byproduct of saponification. *Note: This soap can get quite thick but may resist solidification. Stir to heavy trace before molding and wait until it is quite solid before you remove it from the molds. It is worth the extra effort.* The weights in ounces are indicated in parentheses.

Remember, these are weights, not volumes.

Shocking pink, yellow and green color tabs were used to make this three-layer soap. Divide the batch into three parts, mix the colors and pour it in layers.

INGREDIENTS

350 grams (12.34 ounces) castor oil
650 grams (22.93 ounces) coconut oil
650 grams (22.93 ounces) olive oil
200 grams (7.05 ounces) jojoba oil
650 grams (22.93 ounces) canola oil
50 grams (1.76 ounces) glycerin
342 grams (12 ounces) lye dissolved in 650 grams
    (22.93 ounces) distilled or deionized water

INS: 124
Lye discount as written: 3 percent

Royal Castile Soap

This soap resulted from a challenge to produce a rich, olive oil-heavy, Castile soap without waiting days for it to solidify. Starting with olive oil, we added coconut to boost the lather and then added jojoba oil to counteract the defatting nature of the coconut oil component. The result has a wonderful texture and full floral scent from the essential oils that are added at trace. The weights in ounces are indicated in parentheses.

Remember, these are weights, not volumes.

INGREDIENTS

50 grams (1.76 ounces) beeswax

350 grams (12.35 ounces) olive oil

1300 grams (45.86 ounces) coconut oil

1400 grams (49.38 ounces) soybean oil

300 grams (10.58 ounces) palm oil

684 grams (24 ounces) lye dissolved in

1400 grams (49.38 ounces) distilled or deionized water

This bar normally would be pure white. For visual effect, we divided the batch into portions and made layered soaps. We colored these layers with kelp, cocoa and paprika.

INS: 138
Lye discount as written: 4 percent

Cleopatra's Beauty Bar

Various legends say that Cleopatra's famous beauty was preserved by frequent baths in mare's or ass's milk. Since those are a bit hard to find these days, we substituted nonfat dry milk solids and included shea butter and honey, with just a touch of beeswax. Milk solids and honey are added at trace. Always avoid adding too much honey; it tends to make a sticky soap. The weights in ounces are indicated in parentheses.

Remember, these are weights, not volumes.

We varied this soap bar by embedding a pale green color tab in a shocking pink base. Strawberry fragrance oil adds a complementary scent.

INGREDIENTS

250 grams (8.82 ounces) olive oil

650 grams (22.93 ounces) canola oil

725 grams (25.57 ounces) coconut oil

775 grams (27.34 ounces) palm oil

15 grams (0.53 ounce) shea butter

5 grams (0.18 ounce) beeswax

342 grams (12 ounces) lye dissolved in 700 grams (24.7 ounces) distilled or deionized water

30 grams (1.06 ounces) milk solids

20 grams (0.71 ounce) honey

INS: 151
Lye discount as written: 6.8 percent

Dr. Bob's Facial Soap

Although there is no extra essential or fragrance oil added to this bar, it does tend to smell like an oatmeal cookie when warm. This is very mild chamomile soap with ground oatmeal to exfoliate dead skin cells. At trace, the oatmeal and chamomile are added and, when they are completely combined, the honey is added. The oatmeal is an ideal additive to counteract the tendency of honey to produce a sticky, hard-to-solidify bar. The weights in ounces are indicated in parentheses

Remember, these are weights, not volumes.

This naturally light brown soap, like an oatmeal cookie, is a good candidate for a little cocoa for a darker tint. For optimum effect, embed a pistachio-colored slice.

INGREDIENTS

300 grams (10.58 ounces) olive oil

1450 grams (51.15 ounces) coconut oil

1550 grams (54.67 ounces) palm oil

1310 grams (46.21 ounces) canola oil

15 grams (0.53 ounce) jojoba oil

20 grams (0.71 ounce) shea butter

684 grams (24 ounces) lye dissolved in 1400 grams (39.4 ounces) distilled or deionized water

350 milliliters (1.5 cups) oatmeal, finely ground (preferably regular, not instant)

20 grams (0.71 ounce) chamomile, finely ground

45 grams (1.59 ounces) honey

INS: 152 | Lye discount as written: 3.3 percent

Dr. Bob's Feel Good Soap

Bob's signature herbal soap is made with herbs and essential oils that have a long history of use in herbal medicine to treat various skin insults and injuries. The trick to this bar is adding the vitamin E at trace, before the ground herbs are added. This will help preserve the greenish tint to the bars, which can be enhanced by the addition of chlorophyll or, in this case, powdered kelp. As usual, the aloe-vera gel is added at trace. *Note: Adding the vitamin E after the herbs generally produces a brown bar.* The weights in ounces are indicated in parentheses.

Adding kelp gives this soap a pronounced herbal green color.

Remember, these are weights, not volumes.

INGREDIENTS

300 grams (10.58 ounces) olive oil

1460 grams (51.50 ounces) coconut oil

1560 grams (55.03 ounces) palm oil

1305 grams (46.03 ounces) canola oil

37 grams (1.31 ounces) jojoba oil

684 grams (24 ounces) lye dissolved in 1250 grams (44.1 ounces) distilled or deionized water

30 milliliters (2 tablespoons) vitamin E oil

100 grams (3.53 ounces) aloe-vera gel

19 grams (0.67 ounce) chamomile

18 grams (0.63 ounce) comfrey

17 grams (0.60 ounce) hyssop

14 grams (0.49 ounce) hops

18 grams (0.63 ounce) feverfew

27 grams (0.95 ounce) lavender flowers

30 milliliters (2 tablespoons) kelp powder

30 milliliters (2 tablespoons) lavender essential oil

15 milliliters (1 tablespoon) rosemary essential oil
Note: Two tablespoons equal one ounce.

INS: 152　　|　　Lye discount as written: 3.4 percent

Avocado Green Soap

This recipe springs from the skin-nourishing properties of avocado kernel oil. The amount shown, 200 grams, can be increased to 250 grams for a little additional superfatting for dry skin. Although the recipe is written using shortening, lard may be substituted on an equal weight basis. Lemongrass and kelp (which are added at trace) are considered skin nourishing and provide a nice green color to the bar.

Remember, these are weights, not volumes.

INGREDIENTS

900 grams (31.75 ounces) shortening
500 grams (17.64 ounces) olive oil
700 grams (24.69 ounces) coconut oil
200 grams (7.05 ounces) avocado kernel oil
342 grams (12 ounces) lye dissolved in 700 grams
    (24.7 ounces) distilled or deionized water
15 milliliters (1 tablespoon) lavender essential oil
5 milliliters (1 teaspoon) rosemary essential oil
2.5 milliliters (0.5 teaspoon) vetiver essential oil
30 milliliters (2 tablespoons) dried lemongrass, finely
    ground or 2.5ml (0.5 teaspoon) essential oil
90 milliliters (3 tablespoons) kelp powder
Note: Two tablespoons equal one ounce.

Pigments come in shades as well as colors causing the distinct difference in the two bars on the right. Here we used two different green pigments. The bar on the left is the result of pouring green cold-process soap on top of a red melt-and-pour layer. Let the melt-and-pour completely solidify before pouring the warm cold-process soap on top.

INS: 156
Lye discount as written: 3 percent

Corn Oil Soap

Many common oils found in the grocery store will make a nice bar of soap. Here is one where corn oil has replaced the olive oil. Add scent and color as desired.

Remember, these are weights, not volumes.

INGREDIENTS

600 grams (21.16 ounces) corn oil
200 grams (7.05 ounces) castor oil
600 grams (21.16 ounces) coconut oil
900 grams (31.75 ounces) palm oil
342 grams (12 ounces) lye dissolved in 700 grams
    (24.7 ounces) distilled or deionized water

This bar started with a melt-and-pour layer colored with a gold pearlescent pigment. When solidified, we added the cold-process brick-red pigment-colored soap to fill the mold.

INS: 150
Lye discount as written: 3 percent

Apricot Soap

This recipe has quite a bit of flexibility. Olive oil can be used in place of the canola on an equal weight basis, and the apricot kernel oil can be increased to 250 grams for extra mildness (superfatting). 15ml (½ ounce) of vitamin E can also be added at trace for an extra beneficial touch. To match the composition, turmeric is used to give a peachy color and peach nectar fragrance oil is used for scent.

Remember, these are weights, not volumes.

INGREDIENTS

500 grams (17.64 ounces) canola oil
700 grams (24.69 ounces) coconut oil
900 grams (31.75 ounces) palm oil
200 grams (7.05 ounces) apricot kernel oil
342 grams (12 ounces) lye dissolved in 700 grams (24.7 ounces) distilled or deionized water
30 to 60 milliliters (1 to 2 tablespoons) turmeric
45 milliliters (1.5 ounces) peach fragrance oil
Optional: 15 milliliters (1 tablespoon) vitamin E
Note: Two tablespoons equal one ounce.

This colored bar is not unlike that produced by turmeric, just a little more intense. The deep yellow pigment emphasizes the apricot theme.

INS: 155
Lye discount as written: 3 percent

Abilene Trail Soap

The Abilene Trail was a major route for transporting cattle from the Southwest to market. We created this recipe for those of you who take the time and effort to process your own tallow, as well as the lucky ones who are able to buy refined tallow. It makes a fine hard bar to which you can add a bit of jojoba oil as additional superfat for extra mildness. Sandalwood essential or fragrance oil is a nice touch for the trail boss.

Remember, these are weights, not volumes.

We produced a simple, layered color effect using cold-process soap with pigments. A natural or uncolored base (about half the batch) was poured into the molds. The remainder of the batch was colored with a red pigment and then poured on top of the first layer. To keep the layers separated, the original layer must be thick enough to completely support the subsequent layers.

INS: 157
Lye discount as written: 3 percent

INGREDIENTS

750 grams (26.46 ounces) tallow
950 grams (33.51 ounces) olive oil
600 grams (21.16 ounces) coconut oil
342 grams (12 ounces) lye dissolved in 700 grams (24.7 ounces) distilled or deionized water
30 milliliters (2 tablespoons) sandalwood essential oil
or 45 to 60 milliliters (1.5 to 2 ounces) fragrance oil
Optional: 50 grams (2 ounces) jojoba oil
Note: Two tablespoons equal one ounce.

Sunny Day Soap

This is a nice superfatted (almost 5 percent) soap that contains jojoba, sunflower seed oil, and vitamin E in addition to palm, olive and coconut oils. Add scent and color to please.

Remember, these are weights, not volumes.

INGREDIENTS

675 grams (23.81 ounces) coconut oil

500 grams (17.64 ounces) olive oil

800 grams (28.22 ounces) palm oil

100 grams (3.53 ounces) jojoba oil

300 grams (10.58 ounces) sunflower seed oil

342 grams (12 ounces) lye dissolved in 650 grams
   (22.93 ounces) distilled or deionized water

Add at trace:

15 milliliters (1 tablespoon) vitamin E

A beautiful sunrise effect came from using a natural base at full thick trace with some red pigment soap poured on top. After we poured the red top layer, we used a knife to swirl the colored layer into the plain base. If you use longer molds, you can create a marbled effect by pouring a thick, colored layer into a channel on the surface and then use a knife to create color swirls.

INS: 153
Lye discount as written: 4.8 percent

Luscious Luxury Bar

This is a very special luxurious moisturizing soap containing jojoba oil, lanolin, a lot of olive oil, vitamin E for a special skin treat and a bit of beeswax to keep it long lasting (and to speed up the time to trace). Some people are allergic to lanolin — be sure that you label the lanolin content. For an extra special touch, add a bit of aloe-vera gel and finely ground chamomile flowers at trace.

Remember, these are weights, not volumes.

This example is a hybrid between melt-and-pour and cold-process soap. We started with a thin layer of melt-and-pour soap colored with a gold mica pigment and then added the yellow-pigmented cold-process soap layer.

INS: 154
Lye discount as written: 3 percent

INGREDIENTS

600 grams (21.16 ounces) coconut oil

875 grams (30.86 ounces) olive oil

100 grams (3.53 ounces) jojoba oil

775 grams (27.34 ounces) palm oil

25 grams (0.88 ounce) beeswax

50 grams (1.76 ounces) lanolin

342 grams (12 ounces) lye dissolved in 650 grams
   (22.93 ounces) distilled or deionized water

Add at trace:

15 milliliters (1 tablespoon) vitamin E

Chapter Thirteen: Soap Recipes

Pet Shampoo Bar

This is a favorite recipe of our dog, who's a shepherd, especially after a long weekend at puppy camp (dog kennel) when he needs a little extra tender loving care. It is very mild, with only about 21 percent coconut oil; enough to generate lather but not enough to be especially drying. The shortening is an all-vegetable type. Manuka essential oil can be substituted for the tea tree oil and lemon balm (Melissa) for the clary sage. The aloe-vera gel, vitamin E, ground chamomile, and essential oils are added at trace.

Remember, these are weights, not volumes.

Dogs don't really care what color the soap is; a bath still is an insult to their dignity. However, to please the pet owner, we created lavender- and plum-pigmented bars. Pigments offer the soap maker the ability to produce rich vibrant colors.

INGREDIENTS

100 grams (3.53 ounces) castor oil

500 grams (17.64 ounces) coconut oil

250 grams (8.82 ounces) olive oil

500 grams (17.64 ounces) palm oil

1,000 grams (35.27 ounces) shortening

342 grams (12 ounces) lye dissolved in 650 grams (22.9 ounces) distilled or deionized water

30 milliliters (1 tablespoon) lavender essential oil

60 milliliters (2 tablespoons) tea tree essential oil

5 milliliters (1 teaspoon) rosemary essential oil

2.5 milliliters (0.5 teaspoon) clary sage essential oil

15 milliliters (1 tablespoon) vitamin E

Note: Two tablespoons equal one ounce.

INS: 150
Lye discount as written: 3 percent

Pet Shampoo

If anything, this recipe is even slightly milder than the Pet Shampoo Bar. The essential oil blend of lavender, eucalyptus, cypress and citronella is selected for its insect repellent properties. You can also add pennyroyal and lemongrass or use them to replace, at equal amounts, the citronella and cypress. This might be a good soap to use on a pet who is about to go to puppy camp or who is going to spend some time with you camping.

Remember, these are weights, not volumes.

These blue- and green-pigmented bars were made from the same batch. We separated a small amount of the soap mixture for a separate color treatment and then drizzled it over the top of the blue soap. Since the bottom of the mold yields a smoother soap than the open top, the added color ends up on the bottom of the finished bar.

INS: 152
Lye discount as written: 3 percent

INGREDIENTS

500 grams (17.64 ounces) coconut oil

350 grams (12.35 ounces) olive oil

600 grams (21.16 ounces) palm oil

900 grams (31.75 ounces) shortening

342 grams (12 ounces) lye dissolved in 700 grams (24.7 ounces) distilled or deionized water

15 milliliters (1 tablespoon) lavender essential oil

5 milliliters (1 teaspoon) eucalyptus essential oil

2.5 milliliters (0.5 teaspoon) cypress essential oil

2.5 milliliters (0.5 teaspoon) citronella essential oil

Note: Two tablespoons equal one ounce.

Chapter Thirteen: Soap Recipes

Chapter Fourteen

ESSENTIAL OILS FRAGRANCE GUIDE

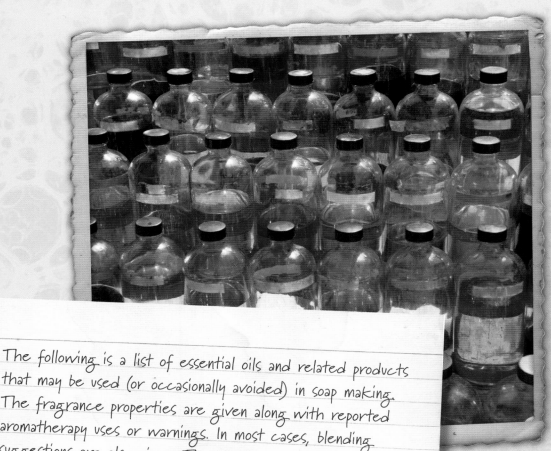

The following is a list of essential oils and related products that may be used (or occasionally avoided) in soap making. The fragrance properties are given along with reported aromatherapy uses or warnings. In most cases, blending suggestions are also given. The chemical constituents are listed to give those familiar with chemistry a hint of the stability under saponification conditions.

ALLSPICE OR PIMENTO: *(Pimenta officinalis).* Warm, spicy, penetrating aroma similar to cloves. Used to increase circulation, relieve tiredness and exhaustion. Blend with lavender, lemongrass, nutmeg. May cause seizing in soap.

ALOE VERA: Known to the Greeks in the fourth century. Used to heal burns, it is typically used as a gel; should be added at trace or rebatch. No fragrance, just nice to the skin. No note.

Aloe vera grows well indoors in pots. Move it outdoors in the summer, but protect it from direct sunlight.

AMBER: Not exactly an essential oil as it is obtained from the destructive distillation of amber, which is a fossilized exudate of some pine trees. However, it is a staple in perfumery and has a penetrating, exotic, uplifting aroma. Contains a complex mixture of terpenes. Mostly middle notes, though we have seen it listed variously as base, middle and middle to top, probably reflecting the variability of the material, depending on the source.

ANGELICA: *(Angelica archangelica).* Rich herbal or earthy aroma. Once thought to be an antidote to bubonic plague, it is part of the flavor system of Chartreuse and Benedictine. Could be photo toxic (causing skin irritation if exposed to the sun). Used in treatments for headache, asthma and stress relief and also has a reputation for healing scars and bruises. Recommended with basil, chamomile, geranium, lavender and citrus. Contains borneol, linalool, bergaptene, limonene, phellandrene and pinene. Top note.

ANISE: *(Pimpinella anisum).* Often used as a flavoring for liqueurs, candies and baked goods due to its intense licorice flavor and taste and its carminative properties. Once used as an aphrodisiac, a reputation that modern studies may support, since it is proven sensually appealing to women. Contains up to 90 percent anethole plus anisaldehyde and methylchavicol. Middle to top notes.

BASIL: *(Ocimum basilicum).* Sweet, spicy fragrance with balsamic notes. Basil is taken from *basilikon phuton*, Greek for kingly herb. Antibacterial; used to clear head from colds and ease headache; used against melancholy and depression in the Middle Ages; used against stress and insomnia; considered an aphrodisiac by the Romans; reported to soothe insect bites. Recommended with bergamot, clary sage, geranium, hyssop, lavender, melissa, sandalwood, verbena. Contains linalool (40 percent to 50 percent), methyl chavicol (24 percent), eucalyptol and estragol. Middle to top notes.

BALM: (lemon) *(Melissa officinalis).* Lemony aroma. The modern name, Melissa, is from the Greek *melissophyllon*, bee leaf, since Melissa is the Greek word for honeybee. Lemon balm is a shortened form of lemon balsam, from the Hebrew *bal-smin*, meaning chief of oils. It is a component of benedictine and chartreuse. Antiseptic properties promote healing of wounds, especially cuts. Used against headaches, depression, anxiety and insomnia. Reputedly antifungal. Blends well with lavender, rose and various citrus. Contains citronellal and geranial plus neral, citronellol and citral. Mostly middle notes, just a bit of top character.

Melissa is a hardy perennial in most of the U.S. It has a tendency to spread and choke other growth.

BAY: (*Pimenta acris, Laurus nobilis*). Powerful spicy aroma, somewhat medicinal. A Roman symbol of wisdom and peace. Contains up to 65 percent to 70 percent phenols (chavicol, eugenol, methyl eugenol) with geraniol, linalool, terpineol, cineol and others. Eugenol alone can account for 40 percent to 55 percent of the oil. Good respiratory aid and topical antiseptic. Used against hair loss. Victorian bay rum was obtained by distilling the leaves in rum. Sweet and spicy aroma, blends well with eucalyptus, juniper, lavender, lemon, rose, rosemary, thyme and ylang-ylang. Base to middle notes.

BOIS DE ROSE: (*Aniba rosaeodora*). Very sweet floral aroma with spicy character. Used

to combat acne, dermatitis, wounds, general skin care (wrinkles, stretch marks and scars). If you are concerned about tropical rainforest destruction, you might try an oil with similar chemical makeup from the Taiwan ho or shiu tree. Contains linalool (up to 97 percent). Blends well with lavender and rose geranium. Middle note.

CAJEPUT: (*Melaleuca cajeputi*). Closely related to the Australian tea tree and naioli oils. Generally used because of the antiseptic properties of the oil, but has some historical usage in herbal treatments for rheumatism and cholera. Although often used undiluted, some allergic reactions recently have been reported. Contains cineol (usually 50 percent to 60 percent), terpineol, pinene. Top note.

CAMPHOR: (cinnamon camphor, white camphor). Cooling oil often used in soaps, disinfectants, etc. Obviously smells like camphor. Blends well with citrus, mint. Contains camphor, terpineol, cineol, pinene, safrol, etc. Middle to top notes.

CARDAMOM: (*Elettaria cardamomum*). Sweet, spicy fragrance; like bitter lemon with woody undertones. One of the oldest known essential oils with reported digestive and aphrodisiac properties. Contains cineol, terpinene, terpineol, borneol, limonene and sabinene as well as linalool and linalyl acetate. Blend with geranium, juniper, lemon, rosewood, verbena. Middle to top notes.

CARROT SEED: (*Daucus carota*). A source of carotene (vitamin A precursor) hence, useful as an antioxidant and in treating skin disorders. Slightly sweet, dry fragrance blends well with citrus, juniper, lavender, rosemary. Contains carotol, asarone, bisabolene, limonene and pinene. Middle note.

CASSIA: (*Cinnamomum cassiac*). From either leaves or bark. Woody, spicy tenacious odor.

Both oils contain cinnamaldehyde (75 percent to 90 percent), methyl eugenol, salicylaldehyde and ethylsalicylaldehyde. Dermal toxin due to cinnamaldehyde content. Should not be used.

CEDAR OIL: (thuja oil) *(Thuja plicata* or *Occidentalis)*. Actually not derived from cedar, but from arbor vitae. Sharp, camphor/evergreen aroma. Contains thujone, an oral toxin, plus fenchone and pinene. Used against plantar warts, poison ivy or oak, and as an insect repellent. It is not recommended for skin contact, but can function to repel insects. Base note.

Arbor vitae, the source of cedar oil, has a wide range of growth zones and often is grown as a windbreak or border.

CEDARWOOD OIL: *(Juniperus virginiani)*. Woody, pine-like aroma. Blends with pine, rose, rosemary, vetiver. Often used to anchor or fix scent blends and is one of the oldest woods used as incense. Blends with cypress and other wood oils as well as patchouli. Used for antiseptic, skin-soothing properties (sometimes applied against cellulite). Has a warm energizing fragrance. Contains cedrene and cedral. Mostly base to middle notes.

CHAMOMILE: Roman *(Anthemis nobilis,* now *Chamaemelum nobile)*. Warm, fruity aroma. Has been in continuous use from the time of the Egyptians, who dedicated it to the gods. Its name is derived from the Greek *chamaimelon,* or apple on the ground, due to its strong apple scent. It is variously recommended for external use against sores, acne, allergies, boils, cuts, eczema, inflammations, rashes, toothaches, migraines, neuralgia, to ease anxiety and treat insomnia. It still is used today in hair preparations to lighten and condition hair. Blends well with angelica, geranium, lavender, lemon, palmarosa, patchouli, rose and ylang-ylang. Contains esters of angelic and tiglic acids (about 85 percent) with pinene, azulene, farnesol and other constituents. Middle to top notes.

CHAMOMILE: German *(Matricaria chamomilla)*. Also called blue chamomile from the characteristic blue color of the azulene, which is formed during steam distillation. Characteristic aroma. See chamomile, Roman. Middle to top notes.

German chamomile is an annual that sometimes will reseed itself. Roman chamomile, shown, is a somewhat tender perennial. The flowers are easy to harvest and dry; and when ground, they make a wonderful addition to soap.

CINNAMON: *(Cinnamomum zeylanicum* or *verum)*. Available from leaves or inner bark. Warm, spicy aroma. Blends well with mandarin (actually most citrus oils) and clove. Leaf contains eugenol (80 percent to 96 percent), cinnamaldehyde (3 percent), linalool, safrol; bark contains cinnamaldehyde (40 percent to

50 percent) eugenol (4 percent to 10 percent), benzaldehyde, pinene, cineol, cymene, others. The bark oil is a dermal toxin and should not be used; the leaf oil should be used with caution as it may cause chemical sensitization. Base to middle notes.

CITRONELLA: (*Cymbopogon nardus*). Powerful, woody, sweet lemony fragrance. Insect repellent and used in Chinese herbal medicine for rheumatic pain relief. Antiseptic, fungicidal action. Composition varies widely depending on place of origin. Contains geraniol (up to 45 percent), citronellol (up to 50 percent) plus geranyl acetate, limonene and camphene. Blend with geranium, citrus, cedar (can be overwhelming). Top note.

CLARY SAGE: (*Salvia sclaria*). Sweet, nutty herbaceous aroma. Blends well with citrus, fir, lavender. Primarily grown as a flavoring for muscatel. In the 16th century, it was considered to be an aphrodisiac. Its name is from the Latin *clarus* for its use to relieve tired, sore eyes. It is also used to combat general fatigue and depression and to condition and darken thinning hair. An ancient Latin saying was *"cur morietur homo, cui salvia crescit in horto?* (How can a man die who has sage growing in his garden?)"* Contains linalyl acetate (up to 75 percent), linalool, pinene and others. Used for acne, wrinkles, muscle aches. Middle to top notes.

CLOVE: (*Eugenia caryophyllata*). The name is from the Latin *clavus*, meaning nail shaped. Strong, spicy penetrating odor. Medicinal history dates to Greeks, Romans, and Chinese. Used to relieve pain, strengthen memory and lift depression. Possible antiseptic for treating skin sores and wounds. Blend with basil, cinnamon, lemon, nutmeg, orange, rosemary. Contains furfural, methyl salicylate, eugenol (82 percent to 87 percent including about 10 percent acetyleugenol), caryophyllene, pinene. May cause soap to seize due to its eugenol content. Middle note.

COFFEE: (coffee *Arabica* and species). Used as essential oil, as strongly brewed coffee or even as finely ground spent coffee grounds. Uplifting characteristic fragrance; often used (in soap) to combat odors on hands and feet; although the coffee aroma fades in soap, it is reportedly still useful in combating odors. Middle note.

COMFREY: (*Symphytum officinale*). Also known as boneset or knitbone. The name is probably from the Roman *conferva*, to join together. It is used against swelling, sprains, bruises, neuralgia and to promote healing of broken bones and sores. Some reports indicate that the mucilage content of its root, used as a poultice, dried to form a mass, which would hold broken bones in place. Contains asparagin. Leaves as well as powdered root are used; not an essential oil. No fragrance notes.

Both the root and the dried leaf of comfrey have medicinal uses. Once established in your garden, it can be hard to contain its vigorous growth.

CYPRESS: (*Cupressus sempervirens*). Refreshing woodsy fragrance. Uses claimed include: deodorant, antiseptic, and insect repellent as well as astringent properties against cellulite and varicose veins. Blends well with various citrus and fir oils. Contains pinene, camphene, terpineol, furfural, cymene, cedrol. Definite middle note.

EUCALYPTUS: (*Eucalyptus globulous*). Sharp and penetrating, spicy camphorous odor. Bactericide, antiviral, insect repellent, parasiticide, burns, pulmonary conditions. Contains eucalyptol or cineole (80 percent to 85 percent), phellandrene, pinene, camphene and others. Blends with coriander, juniper, lavender, lemongrass, Melissa and thyme. Now there are several variants available as essential oils with similar pulmonary effects, but much milder and hence safer, such as lemon eucalyptus (*Eucalyptus citriodora*). Lemon eucalyptus is gaining fame as a skin-friendly mosquito repellent, functional against the mosquito that carries West Nile disease. Top note.

FEVERFEW: (*Chrysanthemum parthenium*). Its name reflects the Latin *febrifugia*, a substance that drives out fevers. Traditionally used to treat fevers, relieve insect bites, calm nerves. It is also used as a moth repellent. Contains camphor. Ordinarily used as ground herb or a tea, not an essential oil. No fragrance notes.

FRANKINCENSE: (*Boswellia thurifera*). Also called *Olibanum* for Lebanon oil. It has a warm spicy woody aroma. It is used as a perfume fixative and incense. Traditional use: to produce a calm, meditative state, ease shortness of breath, etc. Blends well with citrus and exotics and wood fragrances such as patchouli, sandalwood and pine. Contains cadinene, camphene, pinene, phellandrene and olibanol. Middle to base notes.

GERANIUM: (*Pelargonium graveolens* or *Odorantissimum*) "Rose Geranium." Sweet, heavy odor reminiscent of roses. Blends well with lavender, rose and patchouli. Pelargonium is derived from the Greek for stork's bill, reflecting the fruit's shape. To produce a single pound of essential oil, 300 to 500 pounds of plant material are required. It reportedly is an antiseptic and analgesic. Relieves stress, depression, acne, athlete's foot, hemorrhoids, bruises, cuts, burns, dermatitis, etc. Contains

citronellol, geraniol esters (20 percent to 35 percent), linalool, isomenthone, menthone. Blend with angelica, basil, bay, sage, lavender, petitgrain, rose, rosemary and sandalwood. Base to middle notes.

A number of scented geranium varieties are available for the home gardener. They are not hardy, but make good houseplants during the winter.

GUAIACWOOD: (*Bulnesia sarmienti*). Deep, earthy, smoky fragrance. Reported to help tighten and rejuvenate aging skin. Often used with rose-like fragrances and citrus. Contains bulnesol and guaiol. Base notes.

HELICHRYSUM: (*Helichrysum angustifolium*). One of the major essential oils, though there are hundreds of individual species grown. Mostly used for tremendous skin healing properties, this essential oil generally is much too costly for use in soap. Also called Immortelle, Everlasting and Strawflower. Contains geraniol, linalool, nerol and pinene. Middle to top notes.

There are hundreds of Helichrysum species and most are easy-to-grow annuals. Shown is the species strawflower, which produces wonderful healing oil.

HOPS: *(Humulus lupulus)*. Rich, spicy, sweet aroma. Calming and sleep-inducing. Flowers, along with chamomile, are used as a soothing poultice for rheumatic joints. Also against dermatitis, rough skin, asthma, with some reported use in aphrodisiacs (possibly when present with fermented grain extracts). Antimicrobial antiseptic, pleasantly narcotic. For rheumatic joints, neuralgia, antibiotic. Contains 65 percent to 70 percent humulene, myrcene, caryophyllene and farnesene. Middle notes.

HYSSOP: *(Hyssopus officinalis)*. Sweet, penetrating, warm herbal aroma. Flowers attractive to bees. From Hebrew *Ezop*, meaning good scented herb. Eases sprains and rheumatic joints and promotes quick healing of cuts and sores, bruises, dermatitis. Reputed to have a strong therapeutic effect on the mind. Contains about 50 percent pinene, pinocamphone, isopinocamphone, borneol, camphor, thujone, cadinene, others. Blend with angelica, lavender, Melissa, rosemary, tangerine. Middle notes.

Garden-variety hyssop is an easy-to-grow perennial that comes in a variety of colors.

The hops vine is a hardy plant that enjoys creeping up a fence or trellis. The dried flowers are ground and used in beer and soap.

JASMINE: *(Jasminum officinale* and related species and varieties). Available as the absolute or fragrance oil, not true essential oil, although prior to the late 1980s very small quantities of an essential oil were produced. Warm, uplifting, sensuous floral fragrance, called the "king of perfumes or flower oils" with soothing and calming properties. Blend with mandarin, lavender, rose. Contains farnesol, geraniol, nerol, terpineol, jasmone, eugenol. Mostly base notes.

JUNIPER: (*Juniperus communis*). Characterized by the sweet, balsamic odor characteristic of gin. Widespread medicinal use in Tibet, Rome, Greece and Arabia. Used against eczema, acne, sores, ulcers, dermatosis and rheumatism or aching joints. It is an antiseptic and parasiticide. Contains borneol, isoborneol, cadinene, pinene, camphene, terpineol and others. Blends with citrus, geranium, rosemary, sandalwood, various firs. Top and middle notes.

This is a type of juniper readily found in most areas.

LAVANDIN: (*Lavandula fragrans* or *Intermedia*). Aroma similar to lavender, but more penetrating. This hybrid species is a cross between true lavender and aspic, or spike lavender. Whereas lavender is calming and relaxing, lavandin is more stimulating and energizing. A single pound of essential oils is produced from approximately 35 pounds (16kg) of flowers. Contains linalool, linalyl acetate, camphor, cineole, camphene, limonene, etc. Blend with bergamot, chamomile, clary sage, geranium. Middle to top notes.

LAVENDER: (*Lavandula angustifolia*) English Lavender. Floral aroma with woody undertones. From the Latin *lavare*, to wash. Romans added it to their baths for antiseptic and insect repellent properties. Traditional uses include calming nerves, easing sprains and rheumatic pains, and promoting hair growth. Probably due to antiseptic properties,

it is used against abscesses, acne, dermatitis, eczema, insect bites, ringworm, sores, wounds, rheumatism, sprains and especially burns. A 1995 article in the Lancet (a British medical journal) extols the ability of lavender to regulate sleep patterns in people who are being temporarily taken off sleep regulating medication. One of the most important essential oils; 454g (1 pound) of oil is produced from about 45kg (100 pounds) of flowers. Contains up to 40 percent linalyl acetate, linalool, terpineol, limonene, geraniol, cineol, borneol, caryophyllene. Blends with bay, bergamot, chamomile, clary sage, eucalyptus, geranium, nutmeg, patchouli, thyme, rosemary. Definitely middle notes but with base and top notes that can vary depending on year and source.

There are several varieties of lavender available to the home gardener. Check your growth zone carefully for hardiness.

LEMON: (*Citrus limonum*). Refreshing, uplifting, penetrating fragrance. Used for astringent properties and oily skin. Contains limonene, terpinene, citral, linalool, geraniol, and related compounds. Blends well with other citrus fragrances as well as spicy fragrances (clove, cinnamon, cardamom, etc.). Avoid exposure to sunlight after direct contact, due to possible photosensitivity. Contains limonene, terpinene, phellandrene, pinene, citral. Top notes.

LEMONGRASS: (*Cymbopogon citratus*). Strong, lemony aroma, somewhat grassy/

earthy. With rosemary for aches and pains; strongly antiseptic, antibacterial, antifungal; flea and tick repellent. Contains 75 percent to 85 percent citral, citranellal, limonene, dipentene, methylheptanone, farnesol, nerol. Stimulating and revitalizing. Blend with basil, coriander, geranium, lavender, neroli, palmarosa, rosemary, tea tree, litsea cubeba. Middle and top notes.

LILY OF THE VALLEY: (*Convallaria majalis*). Beautiful, clear, floral aroma. Traditionally used to clear the mind or restore memory. Middle note.

LINDEN: (*Tilia europaea*). Sweet, long-lasting aroma. The Linden tree (usually called basswood in the U.S.) is the symbol of the Germanic nation. Contains farnesol. Sleep-promoting, often in combination with hops. Used against burns and blemishes. Blend with lavender, neroli, palmarosa, rose, verbena, violet, ylang-ylang. Available mostly as an extract. Middle note.

The Linden tree or American basswood is noted for its wood used for carving. Its delicate, sweet and fragrant flowers appear in late June or early July.

LITSEA CUBEBA: (*Litsea cubeba*). Essential oil with a very high citral content often added to extend the citrus aroma of other essential oils, which tend not to survive the high alkalinity of saponification. Contains geraniol, linalool, citral, cineole, cadinene, limonene, sabinene. Lemony top notes.

MANUKA: (*Leptospermum coparium*). Also known as New Zealand tea tree. This oil is fairly new to commercialization, although it has been used for centuries by the Maoris for its healing properties. Top note.

MARIGOLD: (*Calendula officinalis*). African or pot marigold. Sharp, herbaceous aroma. Assists the healing of wounds including burns and leg ulcers; smoothing to face and hands (chapped). Contains calendulin (resin) waxes and oil. Not to be confused with the common marigold (*tagetes*). Top note.

The annual Calendula or pot marigold is easy to grow and makes a great border flower. The dried flower heads, source of the essential oil, will give soap a yellow to gold color.

MARJORAM: (*Origanum marjorana*). Warm, woody, spicy and camphorous aroma. Increases circulation, treats bruises; soporific; soothes pain, especially muscles and joints. The Greek goddess Aphrodite supposedly used marjoram to cure the wounds of her son, Aeneus. Contains terpinene, terpineol, borneol, camphor, pinene, caryophylline. Blend with bergamot, chamomile, lavender, nutmeg, rosemary, ylang-ylang. Middle note.

NEROLI OIL: (*Citrus aurantium*). Warm, sweet floral fragrance. Used for skin rejuvenation, sleep aid, relieving chronic anxiety and depression. The prohibitive expense of this essential oil is a result of the yield: it takes about 1,000 pounds of flowers (from the bitter orange tree) to produce one pound of oil. Contains nerol, geraniol, linalool, terpineol, linalyl acetate (7 percent to 18 percent), methyl anthranilate, jasmone, camphene, limonene. Blend with bergamot, coriander, geranium, lavender, palmarosa, petitgrain, rosemary, sandalwood, ylang-ylang. Middle to top notes.

NIAOULI OIL: (see Tea Tree). Clear penetrating camphorous aroma. Strongly antiseptic, it is used for skin irritations and in veterinary medicine as a rub for rheumatic dog limbs. Contains valeric acid, cineole (up to about 65 percent), terpineol, limonene, pinene. Blend with coriander, juniper, lavender, peppermint, rosemary. Top note.

NUTMEG: (*Myristica fragrans*). Sharp spicy aroma. The oil comes from the seed kernel; mace is the husk. Stimulant, hair tonic. This oil is a warming oil and care must be taken to use only small amounts or avoid sensitive skin areas. Contains borneol, geraniol (6 percent), linalool, terpineol, eugenol, safrole, camphene (60 percent to 80 percent), pinene, myristicin (4 percent), elemicin (25 percent). Blend with cinnamon, clove, coriander, Melissa, patchouli, rosemary, tea tree. Middle note.

PALMAROSA: (*Cymbopogon martini*). Sweet, floral aroma with slight rose character. Contains geraniol (75 percent to 95 percent), citronellol, farnesol and others. Used against skin conditions like acne, wrinkles (from sun exposure) and for broken veins. Reputed to refresh and clarify the mind. Contains geraniol, citronellol, farnesol, citral, citronellal, geranyl acetate, limonene. Blend with bergamot, geranium, lavender, Melissa, petitgrain, rosewood, sandalwood, ylang-ylang. Middle note.

PARSLEY: (*Petroselinum sativum*). Grassy, herbal aroma. Used against cystitis, rheumatism, sore eyes, wounds, broken capillaries. Contains terpinene, pinene, apiol and others. Blend with lavender, marjoram, rosemary, thyme, sage and most citrus oils. Top note.

PATCHOULI: (*Pogostemon cablin*). Strong, penetrating sweet, musky and spicy fragrance. Long history of medical use in Malaysia, China, India and Japan and equally long use as an aphrodisiac. It is used as an antiseptic as well as an insecticide. Uses include actions against acne, athlete's foot, dandruff, dermatitis, eczema, sores, wounds. Contains patchouli alcohol (about 40 percent) plus pogostol, bulnesol and others. Blend with bergamot, clary sage, geranium, lavender, lemongrass, neroli, rosewood, peppermint. Base to middle notes.

PEPPERMINT: (*Mentha piperita*). A stimulating and uplifting refreshing fragrance. According to Roman mythology, the nymph Menthe (or Minthe), casualty of an ancient love triangle, was changed into the herb by Pluto. Contains menthol in excess of 50 percent, carvone, menthone, limonene, pulegone, cineol. Blend with juniper, spearmint, patchouli, rosemary, lavender, tea tree. Excessive amounts can be skin irritants. Middle to top notes.

Chocolate mint has a wonderful fragrance.

PETITGRAIN OIL: (*Citrus aurantium*). Fresh floral citrus aroma. Often used in combination with neroli. One of three essential oils from the orange tree, this oil is derived from the leaves. It is reported to clear confusion, depression, mental fatigue. Possible photosensitivity may result if used prior to exposure to sun. Contains (40 percent to 80 percent) linalyl acetate, geraniol, geranyl acetate, limonene. Blend with bergamot, cardamom, geranium, lavender, Melissa, palmarosa, rosemary, rosewood, neroli, ylangylang. Top note.

PINE: (*Pinus sylvestris*). Fresh woodsy fir aroma. Often used for deodorant effect and to increase blood circulation, but can cause skin irritation in high concentration. Contains pinene, cadinene, bornyl acetate, sylvestrene, dipentene. Blends well with cedarwood, sandalwood, guiacwood, cypress. Middle note.

ROSE: (rose otto from *Rosa damascena* and related species). Tremendously uplifting rich floral fragrance, with hundreds of minor chemical components in this oil along with up to 70 percent geraniol. This is one of the oldest (and most expensive) of the essential oils; roughly 4,400 pounds of rose blossoms are needed to produce a single pound of essential oil. Myths relating to roses abound, but it is a noted symbol of silence — a rose suspended over a table was a sign that the discussions held were to be kept secret by all participants, hence the term "sub rosa" (under the rose). Widely used in perfumery and cosmetics both to improve the fragrance bouquet and for the soothing properties to mind and skin. Blend with other floral oils. Middle, plus top and base notes.

This is the prime rose for the distillation of rose otto essential oil. However, many very fragrant varieties are available in the U.S., which can be used for infusion. Photo by Butch Owen.

ROSEMARY: (*Rosmarinus officinalis*). "Dew of the sea" from Corsica and Sardinia. Strong, penetrating, woody, camphorous or balsamic aroma. Used with thyme to treat dandruff. It has been found in the Egyptian tombs, probably as a result of its antioxidant, preservative qualities or possibly due to its use to stimulate and rejuvenate skin. Contains pinenes, camphene, limonene, cineol, borneol (10+ percent), and so on. Used to treat acne, dandruff, eczema, asthma, rheumatism, poor circulation, and to soothe nerves and promote hair growth. Used by Egyptians, Greeks, Romans. Blend with basil, geranium, lavender, lemongrass, Melissa, peppermint, tangerine. Middle to top notes.

SAGE: (*Salvia officinalis*). Warm spicy herbaceous and slightly camphorous aroma. Quickens senses and memory, strengthens sinews. Used for palsy and trembling, rheumatic joints and sciatica, and with chamomile to relieve asthma attacks. Mainly thujone (42 percent) cineol, borneol and other terpenes, it should be used only with caution and is usually replaced by clary sage. Top note.

SANDALWOOD: (*Santalum album*). This oil had to be included since it is such a favorite and has been used in religious rites for centuries, both as incense and even in the construction of temples. Musky rich exotic oil, high-quality fresh oils have little fragrance but reportedly fragrance builds with time and possibly with exposure to air. Used for skin and hair care. Blends well with rose, jasmine, lavender, patchouli and other exotics. Contains forneol, santalone and related compounds. Full of base notes.

SELF HEAL: (*Prunella vulgaris*). Frequently used to stem blood from accidents and fights due to its styptic properties. Not known as an essential oil; used as ground herb or tea. No fragrance notes.

SPEARMINT: (*Mentha viridas*). Warm herbaceous minty aroma. Mild antiseptic, acne, skin irritations, headache, nausea, antidepressant, mental strain, fatigue. Contains (50 percent+) carvone, limonene, pinene. Blends well with peppermint and various citrus oils. Middle to top notes.

SPIKE LAVENDER: (*Lavandula latifolia* or *spica*, also called aspic). Like lavandin, this oil is energizing rather than calming. Traditional uses against rheumatism, arthritis. Contains cineole (ca. 35 percent) and camphor (40 percent to 60 percent) with linalool, borneol, terpineol and camphene. Aroma similar to lavender, but more camphorous. Eases breathing and clears a stuffy head. Blend, as with lavender. Middle and top notes.

TEA TREE: (*Melaleuca alternifolia*). Closely related to cajeput (*Melaleuca cajeputi*) and niaouli (*Melaleuca viridiflora*). Spicy, camphorous, somewhat balsamic odor. Can be blended with lavender, peppermint and fir oils, more to disguise its own odor than enhance the other. Used against abscesses, acne, athlete's foot, herpes, rashes, plantar warts, insect bites, sinusitis, asthma, bronchitis, burns and sunburns, lice, antifungal treatment against tinea, pedis, ringworm, candida. One pound of oil is distilled from about 45 pounds of leaves. Contains terpinene- 4-ol (up to 30 percent), viridiflorene, cineol, pinene, terpinenes, cymene and others. Reportedly absorbed through skin; has anesthetic properties. 1933 British Medical Journal reported it was a powerful disinfectant; 1955 reported in U.S. that it was actively germicidal. Top notes.

THYME: (*Thymus vulgaris*). Powerful warm spicy herbaceous odor. Blends with citrus, lavender, pine, rosemary. Has strong antiseptic properties due to thymol in oil. It has varied uses including the treatment of stuffy nose, fatigue, skin sores and pimples, burns, insect bites, rheumatism and with rosemary for dandruff. Contains thymol and carvacrol (up to 60 percent) with cymene, terpinene, camphene, borneol, linalool and some others. It was used by the Sumarians, Egyptians and Romans, who thought it dispelled melancholy and promoted bravery; it was often carried to prevent airborne diseases. From the Greek *thumos*, for smell or perfume. Middle note.

Grown in the garden or in a pot on the kitchen window, thyme is a wonderful culinary and medicinal herb.

VERBENA OIL: (*Lippia citriodora* or *Aloysia triphylla*). Sweet lemony floral fruity aroma. A South American plant introduced to Europe by the Spanish. It has been used to treat acne and to aid in relaxation. It is especially used with rosemary and lavender. Contains citral (30 percent to 35 percent), geraniol, nerol, others. Possible phototoxicity due to citral content. Top note.

VETIVER OIL: (*Andropogon zizanioides*). Sweet woody earthy fragrance. Moisturizing and stimulates circulation for arthritis. Used for dry, irritated mature or aging skin. Calming and sedating. Contains vetiverols (45 percent to 65 percent), vetivene, 8 percent to 35 percent ketones including vetivones. Often used as a base or fixative for fragrance blends. It takes almost 300 pounds of this grass to produce a single pound of oil. Full base note.

VIOLET FLOWER/LEAF OIL: (*Viola odorata*). Sweet rich floral fragrance. It has been culti-vated for over 2,000 years as a coloring agent and source of perfume. Various reported uses include treatment of skin inflammation, rheumatism, to encourage sleep and relieve headache. Contains saponins, violarutin, methyl salicylate, others. Middle note.

Violets are easy to grow, but the more fragrant varieties are quite tender and not as showy as this species from our shaded part of the garden.

WINTERGREEN: (*Gualtheria promcumbens*). Strong, characteristic minty aroma. Contains mainly methyl salicylate. Can be absorbed through skin and may contribute to salicylate poisoning when overused or used in conjunc-tion with other salicylates, including aspirin. Often used as a counter-irritant in phar-maceutical rubs to draw blood to bruised skin and especially sore joints. Use only with caution. Top note.

YLANG-YLANG: (*Cananga odorata*). "Flower of flowers," "queen of perfumes" (and poor man's jasmine as well). Pronounced ee-long, ee-long. Intensely sweet, floral, somewhat spicy aroma. We found these flower buds used in both Taiwan and Thailand in strings to be hung in automobiles as natural air fresheners. In Thailand they were strung together in long strands with rose petals and jasmine buds. Wow! Used as part of dry-scalp treatment and for dry aging skin. Antidepressant, antiseptic, aphrodisiac, insomnia, relief of nervous depression, anxiety. Also includes other various reported uses: treatment of skin inflammation, rheumatism, to encourage sleep and relieve headache. Ylang-ylang often is available in several varieties, referring to how it is distilled as well as the quality of the oil. Do not be surprised to see something called ylang-ylang II (or 2) or III (3); each version is a bit different, so evaluate the cost and the scent of each. Personally, we think a good soap would be one scented with ylang-ylang and containing witch hazel (obviously, would be called ylangylang, the witch is dead soap). Contains geraniol and linalool acetates and benzoates, cadinenes, pcresol methyl ether. Blends well with lavender, rosemary and other florals. It has been cultivated for over 2,000 years as a coloring agent and source of perfume. Contains saponins, violarutin, methyl salicylate, others. Middle note.

— Chapter Fifteen —
FREQUENTLY ASKED QUESTIONS

Over the years and through as many classes as we have taught there seem to be some questions that arise almost without fail. We have tried to answer the bulk of them here. Questions are good and lead to wonderful discoveries but these answers are meant to help along the way and provide a little clarity.

What does the term hand-milled mean?

Milling is a common industrial term that basically means "ground." Hand-milled soap is soap that is ground (or grated) by hand and then reassembled into bar form. Ground or grated soap is easier to dissolve in water or milk than a big lump. There is no real difference between hand-milled and rebatched soap; it is just a matter of semantics. On the other hand, *French milled* generally refers to soap that has been pressed through steel rollers under relatively high pressure. This softens the soap during processing and enables the production of a smoother, almost plastic feeling soap. A comparable effect can often be obtained by allowing CP or HP soap to go through the gel phase.

I want to start my own business and think that selling my soap would be a natural. Don't you agree?

It depends. We would bet that the failure rate of small soap businesses is about the same as for any other small business. If you want to make soap and generate enough income to pay for supplies — yes, you probably can start a business. If you wish to grow your business into a $50,000 a year (or better) job, it will depend on your dedication, marketing, financing and business sense. There are several decent books available that offer advice for starting your own business — what you need, how much cash reserve, licensing and insurance, business plan, etc. Start with a tax number, usually obtained by writing or calling your state department of revenue. Check into zoning and similar legal restrictions on cottage industries. Decide whether you wish to incorporate, form a partnership or form a single-owner business.

Think about liability insurance. Think about advertising. Think about wrapping and the cost of packaging that can run as much as the cost of ingredients. These all are part of a good business plan. Finally, think about operating at a loss for two years and whether you can afford that. Get competent financial and legal advice. The first step is to determine just what your soap costs you. What are the raw-ingredient costs now, including delivery, and what would they be at the next level up in scale?

Once you determine your cost per bar (or pound or loaf), including packaging, then you need to determine the price per bar. It would be nice to use a formula multiplying your time by so much per hour, but the reality is that there is a market established and you will compete in and with this market. Anyway, when you have cost and price you can determine the gross margin per unit price, less cost.

If you have to rent a facility to make soap or a store to sell it, that will change the picture, but for the moment, leave it as it is and go to the next step.

How much per month do you want or need to make? This is up to you to decide. Let's say the answer is $2,000 per month. Divide your gross margin into $2,000 and this is the number of bars or units you will need to sell each month on average, assuming no additional overhead. The final step in this abbreviated process relates to cost of sales, which often is difficult to determine ahead of time on a unit basis. This would be extra costs to rent a place to sell your soap, or gas and maintenance on a car to visit potential clients, or extra costs for lights, water, insurance, phone, a computer presence, ads in newspapers or magazines. Add up all these costs (per month) and again divide by the gross margin. This gives you the number of extra units you have to sell each month to recover your hidden costs. Can you do it? Or perhaps, how can you do it?

Here are the basics you need to put into your business plan:

- Do you have enough money to build and maintain inventory? You can't just take an order and then make enough soap to fill it. You need a reasonable turnaround time and that means finished soap as well as the raw materials for replacing what you sell. You probably will need to stock at least a one-month supply (or better, a two-month supply) of soap to cover irregular order patterns. And not just today.

- What if your business expands? Can you do it all yourself and in the same location?

- Do you need employees and what will that cost and how will that affect the cost and gross margin per unit?

- What about time? Did you go into business for yourself to be at home with the family; realize your personal potential; be your own boss? Realistically, you need to consider the time you have that you are willing, long-term, to put into the business. If it becomes apparent that time demands exceed your willingness to spend the time, you have a problem. One that perhaps can be solved by hiring employees, taking on a partner, getting the family involved in the business, too. There are many ways to handle this issue, just don't let the problem take you by surprise. Plan ahead.

- You like making soap — you like soap — you like having your own business. Do you like selling, bookkeeping and accounting? Not everyone is comfortable marketing and selling his or her product to the general public. Not everyone is organized or self-disciplined enough to keep track of taxes, revenue, expenses, etc. Take the time to evaluate yourself and be sure that you are willing to deal with all phases of running your own business. If you can do all of that, we'll probably see your soap in the stores very soon.

Will I have to buy a lot of expensive equipment to make soap?

No. In fact, most "soapers" get started with common kitchen equipment. A candy thermometer, steel pot or crockpot, steel or plastic spoon, heat-resistant measuring cup and some sort of a scale are the basics. Personally, we would invest in a stick blender. Used carefully, the stick blender cuts the batch time to a minimum and can be easily cleaned. Even the molds don't have to be expensive — most plastic bins, bowls or drawer dividers can be pressed into service, though silicone molds are readily available.

Can I use my cookie cutters and muffin molds for soap?

Cookie cutters generally can be used without a problem, since you are cutting finished soap with little or no lye remaining. Muffin molds can be used for melt-and-pour soap and probably for rebatched soap without any problems. However, if the molds are aluminum, they will be attacked by cold-process soap and will discolor the surface of the soap, indicating that some of the aluminum is being eaten away. Other alternatives are readily available; it is best to avoid all aluminum molds for cold-process soap.

What's the difference between an oil, fat, essential oil and fragrance oil?

If you are confused by these terms, you're not alone. Most new soap makers ask about the differences. Oils and fats both are normally bland-smelling materials composed of glycerin and fatty acids, but fats come from animals while oils are from vegetable sources. Both oils and fats react with lye to form a fatty-acid salt, which we just call soap, plus glycerin. Essential and fragrance oils do not form soap; they are mixtures of fragrant natural or synthetic chemicals. Essential and fragrance oils do not require any adjustment in your soap recipes unless your scent specifically says it contains some vegetable oil in addition to the fragrance material.

I have heard something about citrus oils being phototoxic; is it true?

Some essential oils contain a class of compounds known as coumarins that are suspected to cause skin sensitization and, on subsequent exposure to the sun, promote sunburning and burn-like skin reactions. Citrus oils, except for sweet orange, grapefruit and mandarin, must be used with caution or avoided before sun exposure. Since soap essentially is washed away with the rinse water, there is question as to the danger involved in using other citrus oils as scents.

Lye seems so harsh. Is there any way to make soap without it?

Part of what makes lye harsh is also what enables it to react with fats and oils to form soap. Good soap, however, should not have any lye remaining in it; all the lye should be consumed or used by the fats and oils, making soap. It would be misleading to see a list of soap ingredients showing lye as an ingredient, since if the soap is well-made, there should be no residual lye in it. It is possible to make soap without lye, but this ordinarily would require purchasing fatty acids rather than fats and oils. Fatty acids are not widely available to home soap makers.

Can I use food coloring to color my soap?

Food colorings available in grocery stores ordinarily are considered too diluted to effectively color soap. Not all food colors are stable in soap either — the color may disappear or change to a different color altogether. Although it is not a huge defect, many dyes are not light stable, meaning they will fade if left in the sun. If you are looking for a light color tint with a small batch of soap, you might try food colors, but we would not recommend scaling up to several pounds without trying it on just a few bars first. For best results, use the dye concentrates.

How can I make a really white bar of soap? Can I use bleach with the ingredients?

Your soap usually will be a natural white as long as you use very light vegetable oils and fats. If your ingredients are green (such as a dark olive oil or pumice) or yellow (such as some palm oils with added carotene), then your soap will be anything from beige, a very pale green or a yellow. If you want the soap whiter you can add titanium dioxide, a very white opaque pigment, which commonly is used in soaps. We do not recommend using chlorine bleach to decolorize your oils. The chlorine can react to form chlorinated organic materials, which may cause allergic skin reactions. If you really need to try bleaching your fats or oils, you could try 3 percent hydrogen peroxide, commonly available in most pharmacies or supermarkets. Weigh out the fats and oils in your recipe and add 3 to 5 grams of 3 percent hydrogen peroxide per 454g (1 pound) of fat or oil as you start melting them together. It doesn't seem like a lot, but adding more rarely will help.

What is the best way to color cold-process soap?

The answer really depends on what sort of effect you are trying to achieve. The most vivid colors usually result by adding pigment colors to the soap. Pigments make it easy to add splashes of bright color by pigmenting part of a batch and adding that in "dollops" to the mold containing uncolored soap. If you are looking for a more subdued "natural" appearance, uniform throughout the bar, then you probably should start with natural vegetable colors. Dyes usually are the best color choice for melt-and-pour and are very user-friendly with rebatched soap, but are a little less predictable and take a bit more cautious experimentation in cold-

process soap. However, if you are looking for unusual visual effects, choose a more luminous colorant.

What does "trace" mean?

We use the common term "tracing," which is a sign that the soap mixture has become a stable emulsion and is ready to pour into molds. The solution is considered at trace when you take a spoonful out of the pot and pour it back in and you can see a faint impression remaining briefly on the surface of the liquid where the liquid went in. Those of you who are proficient cooks can, with a little practice, determine visually when a stable emulsion has formed. If you get confused about trace, think thick, but pourable. The soap should not settle readily into layers when you stop stirring it. Some of our favorite batches looked like pudding as we poured the soap into the molds.

How can I explain the uneven surface finish of the soap?

Here is a description we wrote that describes the finished appearance. Feel free to adapt it to your own special soap: As the batch saponifies (converts), fine oils are added to impart fragrance and other desired special properties. The still-liquid soap is then poured into small molds to solidify. Each batch is unique and the surface of the finished soap reflects the hand processing. Color and surface vary from batch to batch and from mold to mold as small differences in cooling temperatures and rates produce a unique surface. Hand finishing completes the process so that each bar is truly hand crafted from our hands to your hands.

What's that white stuff on the surface of my soap?

The composition of a white surface layer (usually called ash) that sometimes occurs on soap is a matter of debate. Soap actually can exist in any of four interchangeable crystalline forms. Which type of crystal forms depends on a variety of factors, such as the temperature where the crystals form and the amount of water in the mix. The physical description of one particular form, designated as the "beta" form, seems to match the physical properties of what we usually call "ash." At least one soap maker, has had her ash layer analyzed by an outside laboratory and only soap was found. This supports the likelihood that most ash really is just another form of soap crystal. The often expressed observation that rebatched or Castile (100-percent olive oil) soap bars have a different texture, also indicates (at least to us) that we often create these different crystal structures (called polymorphs if you must know) without realizing it. We have noticed that soap that obviously goes through the gel phase rarely develops this white surface material. This also supports the theory that the white material is a crystalline form of soap that forms only under specific temperature conditions. The term ash rightly refers to sodium carbonate, which can form from exposure of excess lye (in soap) to the air.

When has the soap reaction finished?

Saponification definitely is not finished when the liquid soap is poured into the mold. The actual completion time depends on too many factors to generalize; usually it is complete after 24 hours. There is some compelling evidence that HP soap finished in the oven is virtually complete after about two hours in the oven. At cooler temperatures, completion of saponification requires resting overnight, about 12 to 15 hours. However, an appreciable amount of water must still evaporate before the soap is hard enough to put into use.

How do I add silk to my soap?

To achieve a truly "silky" feeling soap, you can add silk to your soap. The easiest way to add silk protein is to add a few small pieces of silk to the lye solution right after it is mixed. Although you may have to push the silk down into the lye solution with a spoon until it gets thoroughly wet, it should dissolve fairly readily. Then, use this solution to make your soap. Various suppliers also offer silk proteins that can be added directly to your soap or shampoo.

Can I use my favorite perfume or after-shave to scent my soap?

You might be able to do it, but since both types of scent have a fairly high alcohol content, you may run the risk of seizing your soap before you add enough to give your soap an appreciable fragrance.

How do I use the information on essential oils and herbs to make a pet shampoo or flea-repellent shampoo?

Using any plain soap is a good way to start, but add a few drops of lavender and/or tea tree oil to the rinse water. These oils normally are well tolerated and good for the skin. But the general approach for formulating functional soaps is to look at the list of essential oils and note how they have been used. Lavender, tea tree or manuka, rosemary, clary sage, chamomile and lemon balm (Melissa) all have been used to treat various skin problems. Therefore, a soap containing several of these oils would be a good place to start. Similarly, lavender, eucalyptus, lemongrass, cypress, citranella and pennyroyal have been used to repel insects such as fleas. In this case, you would want a repellent blend that is not offensive to you if your freshly bathed pet sits down near you. To us, that means don't add too much citronella, which is quite pungent. We include specific blends in Chapter 13, Soap Recipes.

What fragrances are most popular?

Obviously the answer depends on your audience. Following, we've listed the most popular essential oils, selected by over 100 people working in, or familiar with, the field of aromatherapy.

1. Lavender
2. Sandalwood
3. Peppermint
4. Eucalyptus
5. Rosemary
6. Tea tree
7. Geranium
8. Rose
9. Citrus (bergamot, lemon, neroli, grapefruit, orange, tangerine, lime)
10. Clary sage
11. Frankincense
12. Patchouli
13. Chamomile

These selections reflect a combination of beneficial properties, which include, but by no means are limited to, aroma. Although, we can say that these reflect the most requested fragrances available as herbs and essential oils.

Dr. Bob's Favorite Blends

These are Dr. Bob's favorite fragrance blends that only require two or three scents. The numbers refer to drops of each scent in the blend. And remember — rose blends with almost anything and almost everything blends with rose.

1. Luscious lavender: 3 lavender; 1 rosemary
2. JuicyMint: 3 grapefruit; 1 spearmint
3. Timeless: 3 patchouli; 1 peppermint
4. Plenty-Good: 3 cucumber; 1 anise
5. Holiday Punch: 2 cinnamon; 1 orange
6. DublMint: 2 peppermint; 1 spearmint
7. English Garden: 2 to 3 lavender; 1 rosewood
8. Mint Patty: 2 to 3 chocolate; 1 peppermint
9. Wink: 3 juniper berry; 1 grapefruit or bergamot
10. Peppy Mint: 4 tea tree; 1 peppermint
11. Royal Bouquet: 4 ylang-ylang II; 2 lavender; 1 palmarosa; 1 rosemary
12. Pine Barrens: 3 white pine; 1 cypress; 1 cedarwood; 0.5 guaiac
13. Lavender Rose: 4 lavender; 1 palmarosa; 1 rosewood
14. Herb Garden: 4 rosemary; 1 thyme; 1 clary sage
15. Heaven Scent: 4 ylang-ylang II; 1 jasmine; 0.5 to 1 rose
16. Chocolate Chip Cookie: 2 brown sugar; 1 vanilla; 0.5 chocolate
17. Blueberry Muffin: 2 brown sugar; 1 vanilla; 0.5 blueberry

My butcher can give me tallow for almost nothing. What do I need to do to it before I can use it in soap?

Tallow, hard beef fat, needs to be purified or rendered before use in soap. One of the easiest ways we know is to put the tallow in a large stockpot and add approximately 237ml (1 cup) of water and 58g (3 tablespoons) salt for every 454g (1 pound) of tallow. Bring this to a boil, and keep it boiling for a half hour. Cool it to room temperature, and place it in the refrigerator until the top tallow layer has solidified. Remove this solid tallow and scrape off any dark material on the bottom (this will be meat residue and other proteinaceous material). We recommend taking this top layer and repeating the boiling and cooling treatment, this time using 237ml (1 cup) water and 30g to 45g (2 to 3 tablespoons) baking soda per 454g (1 pound). This solid layer now can be used for soap. Keep it refrigerated or frozen if you do not plan to use it right away — it will spoil. See additional ways to render tallow (fat) on page 92.

Why do I have to weigh all my ingredients?

Chemical reactions, such as saponification, are based on the molecular weights of all the chemicals that react. Measuring cups and similar volume-measuring devices are not accurate enough to assure that the correct amounts of the ingredients are used. Since lye is very harsh, it is important to be sure the correct amount is used in a recipe and this means weighing the ingredients. In fact, you should weigh most ingredients in grams as opposed to ounces since grams are metric units.

How do I make bath salts to go with my soap?

Bath salts are pretty simple to make, and you have several choices. Basically, they are composed of one or more Epsom salts, sea salt and baking soda. If baking soda is used, it generally is no more than about 1/3 of the total. Ideally, all components will have about the same particle size so you don't have big crystals of sea salt and fine, powdered baking soda; the fine stuff will tend to separate from the coarse over time. Once you have your blend of salts, add about 5ml (1 teaspoon) essential oil per 453g (1 pound) and you will have a nice fragrant bath salt.

I want to make enough lye solution for several batches. Can I store and reheat lye?

You can store and reheat lye but **always make sure no one will mistake the lye solution for ordinary water while it's being stored.** Cover the lye solution with a lid or something like plastic wrap to keep it airtight. You can reheat lye by placing it in a pan of warm water. We cannot recommend trying to heat it in a microwave; it could easily boil over and give you a dangerous mess to clean up. Make sure that any glass or plastic item used to store and heat lye is in good shape, without cracks or chips. Finally, consider that it often is not necessary to heat lye water above room temperature.

Will castor oil make my soap lather better?

Many people ask about adding castor oil to soap to improve the amount of lather. Castor oil itself does not add to the amount of lather, only the soap made from castor oil is effective. To achieve full effect, castor oil should be present at the start of saponification, not added at trace as to superfat. If you really want to make a thicker, more luxurious, longer-lasting lather, try adding extra glycerin to the mixture at almost any point during saponification. Glycerin essentially produces stronger bubbles, which resist thinning and breaking. Thus, the lather becomes longer lasting and thicker.

How do I make laundry soap?

In the past, laundry soaps often came in bar form. These bars usually were a mixture of soap and 50 percent washing soda (sodium carbonate, not baking soda, which is sodium bicarbonate). Laundry soaps that were yellow also contained rosin, probably 1 percent to 2 percent of the bar. Since laundry soaps didn't need to be formulated to do anything other than clean clothing, they usually were made from coconut oil (for suds) and tallow. Although, today, you could add sodium carbonate to your soap at trace. It really would be easier to make a simple soap, grate it, and add washing soda to the wash water separately. Let the grated soap dissolve in the wash water before adding clothes to avoid creating a gummy mess (undissolved soap) on your clothing.

I found a recipe I want to try, but it is too large. What do I do?

In general, recipes can be scaled up or down with few problems. If you cut all amounts (lye, water and oils) in the recipe by half, the proportions will still be good. When you are decreasing the size of a recipe, you frequently need to increase the temperatures of the oils by five or so degrees and, when you increase the size, you should decrease the temperatures by the same five degrees. This allows for an increase or decrease in the rate at which heat is lost during your soap making.

GLOSSARY

Don't panic! You don't need to know or understand all of these terms to successfully make soap. They are presented here to provide you with a greater understanding of the terms used in this book and to help you when purchasing materials for your soap making.

AFRICAN BLACK SOAP: A natural soap made in various regions of Africa using un-refined shea butter and the ash from various indigenous plants as the source of alkali. The soap is said to have remarkable skin healing properties.

ANTIOXIDANT: A synthetic chemical or natural material that prevents or slows oxidation and rancidity in oils and soaps.

ABSOLUTE: A fragrance extract made by extracting a concrete with alcohol.

ALDEHYDE: A class of chemical compounds containing carbon, hydrogen, and oxygen. Aldehydes are more volatile and more reactive or unstable than alcohols, especially in the presence of strong alkali (lye).

AROMATHERAPY: A theory that bodily health can be affected though the use of essential oils applied to the skin and/or inhaled to directly stimulate the brain to alter one's mental state or improve the healthful function of other bodily systems.

ASH: a) A common term for a loose white layer that often forms at the surface of cold-process soap, consisting of either sodium carbonate (from the reaction of lye with carbon dioxide from the air) or loose "beta" type soap crystals. b) The residue from burning hardwood, from which a form of lye can be extracted.

CASTOR OIL: Inedible oil derived from the castor bean. It is high in ricinoleic acid, which contains a hydroxy group (-OH). It often is used in shampoo soap formulations.

CASTILE: Olive oil-based soap. The term often is used to describe both 100-percent olive oil-based soap as well as soap made primarily, but not exclusively, with olive oil.

COLD PROCESS: A process where fats and oils are converted to soap without cooking. Once the oils are heated to a desired temperature, a lye and water solution is added while stirring, and the oils are converted to soap plus glycerin. The reaction temperature is often at or near room temperature as long as the oils are liquid.

COLORANT: Natural or synthetic materials such as dyes, pigments and herbs used to impart color to soap.

COMBAR: Short for combination bar. Many commercial bar "soaps" are combinations of soap plus synthetic detergent.

CONCRETE: Fragrance extract, usually of a flower, made by extracting the fragrance components into hexane or a similar organic solvent.

DETERGENT: Blend of surfactants, usually synthetic, designed for cleaning, especially in the laundry; also a synthetic surfactant.

DREADED ORANGE SPOTS: Dark spots, usually orange or yellow, that form on the surface of soap caused by the oxidation of the component oils. Superfatted soaps are especially susceptible to this unless an antioxidant is added.

EMBOSSED: Soap that has a type of bas-relief surface. The embossing can be stamped using high-pressure dyes on finished soap or by casting soap over a rubber sheet containing the embossing pattern.

EMOLLIENT: A material that has a soothing, softening effect on skin.

EMULSION: A stable, non-separating suspension of oil in water or water in oil.

ENFLEURAGE: A French term for the extraction of fragrance from flowers or herbs into oil.

ESSENTIAL OILS: Essential oils are prepared from herbs and flowers either by steam distillation or by cold-pressing (squeezing) oils from citrus peel. Essential oils are thought to have both mental and physical therapeutic effects.

ESTER: A type of neutral compound formed by a condensation reaction between an acid and an alcohol. Chemically, fats and oils are esters of glycerin and fatty acids.

FAT: Similar in composition to vegetable oils, but sourced from animals. Fats are neutral compounds (esters) of glycerin and fatty acids.

FATTY ACID: An organic acid produced in plants and animals, usually containing an even number (at least eight) of carbon atoms. Chemically, a fatty acid is composed of carbon, hydrogen and oxygen.

FATTY ALCOHOL: A neutral fatty material containing an alcohol functional group. Most fatty alcohols are synthesized from fatty-acid esters, although they occasionally occur in plants and animals.

FOOD, DRUG AND COSMETIC (FD&C): Materials listed as approved by the federal government for use in foods, drugs or cosmetics.

GLYCERIN: A natural three-carbon liquid sugar that forms the backbone of fats and oils.

GMS: Goat's milk soap.

GSE: Grapefruit-seed extract; thought to be an antioxidant.

HOT PROCESS: A method for making soap that involves continuous cooking (heating) of the reaction mixture, often in a crockpot or oven.

HPCP (or sometimes CPHP): Hot-process soap making using a crockpot.

HYDROPHILIC: Water-loving. Hydrophilic material tends to absorb or dissolve in water.

INFUSION: A tea-like extract of plant matter in either water or oil. Herbs and flowers are steeped or marinated in liquid to produce an infusion.

INS: A term that relates oil to the properties of soap made from that oil. INS relates to both the degree of unsaturation and the size (molecular weight) of the oil. In conventional soap products, Lever Brothers was able to demonstrate a correlation between INS and consumer preference since it reflects compositions that relate to lather and mildness.

IODINE VALUE: A measure of the un-saturation of a fat or oil. It is experimentally determined (measured).

KETONE: A type of neutral organic compound containing a carbon-oxygen double bond. Ketones are fairly stable and usually more volatile than their corresponding alcohols.

KOH: The chemical formula for potassium hydroxide. KOH produces soap that is substantially more soluble than sodium-based soaps. As such, it finds use in both transparent and liquid soaps.

LAURIC ACID: A fatty acid, 12 carbon atoms in length. Lauric-acid soaps foam highly and readily dissolve grease and oil.

LINOLEIC ACID: A polyunsaturated fatty acid, 18 carbon atoms in length. It is more unsaturated than linoleic acid and much more likely to oxidize and become rancid.

LIPID: A fat or fatty material.

LIPOPHILIC: Fat-loving. The fatty tails of a soap molecule are lipophilic, while the acid group at the "head" of the molecule is hydrophilic.

LYE: The common name for sodium hydroxide. In the past, it referred to natural alkaline material leached from wood ash and used to make soap; in that sense it also can refer to potassium hydroxide and its solutions.

LYE DEMAND: The amount of lye needed to completely saponify a fat or oil.

LYE DISCOUNT: The amount of lye omitted from a soap recipe in order to assure an excess of fat or oil (i.e. in order to superfat).

MELT-AND-POUR: A type of soap, usually transparent, which when heated will melt and then solidify again upon cooling. Often seen shortened to M&P.

MYRISTIC ACID: A fatty acid, 14 carbon atoms in length. Together with the 12-carbon lauric acid, it is primarily responsible for lather production in soap.

NaOH: Sodium hydroxide — ordinary lye.

OCCLUSIVE: Blocking the evaporation of water, usually from the skin.

OIL: Triglyceride (compound comprised of glycerin and fatty acids) from vegetable sources.

OLEIC ACID: An 18-carbon (length) fatty acid with a single double bond (unsaturation). The chief fatty acid in olive oil.

OLEFIN: A generic term for organic compounds, hydrocarbons, which are unsaturated (have at least one carbon-carbon double bond in the molecule).

OXIDATION: A chemical reaction with oxygen. Rust is an oxidation product of iron; rancidity or orange spots are caused by the oxidation of polyunsaturated fatty acids.

PALMITIC ACID: Fully saturated fatty acid, 16 carbons in length. The main fatty acid in palm oil.

pH: A scale, from zero to 14, which measures the acidity or alkalinity of water. A pH of 7 is neutral, below 7 is acidic; above is alkaline.

PHOTOTOXIC: Causing a toxic reaction, usually on the skin, when exposed to sunlight.

PIGMENT: Natural or synthetic inorganic colors, often oxides of metallic elements.

POLYMORPH(IC): One of several naturally occurring crystalline structures of the same material, often exhibiting dissimilar physical properties.

POLYUNSATURATED: Having more than a single carbon-carbon double bond in a molecule. Polyunsaturated oils are more liquid (have a lower freezing point) than saturated oils and also more prone to oxidation. Linseed oil, highly polyunsaturated, can cause fires when left exposed to air due to the heat liberated by air oxidation.

RANCID: Degraded by oxidation. In the extreme case, oils become cloudy and smelly due to air oxidation.

REBATCHING: Preparation of soap by redissolving freshly made soap in water or milk and allowing it to crystallize again.

RICINOLEIC ACID: Unique to castor oil, this 18-carbon fatty acid is monounsaturated (like oleic) with an additional alcohol, functional group along the chain.

ROE: Rosemary oil extract or rosemary oleoresin extract. A fat-soluble antioxidant extracted from rosemary with proven antioxidant applications. Virtually all of its proven antioxidant properties are derived from the chemicals carnosol and carnosic acid, which are complex polycyclic compounds containing 20 carbon atoms. ROE should contain at least 7 percent carnosic acid.

SAPONIFICATION: The chemical reaction between lye and fats or oils, yielding soap and glycerin as the products of the reaction.

SAP: Short for saponification value. The amount of lye required to completely saponify a specific amount of fat or oil.

SATURATED: Containing the maximum amount of hydrogen, therefore without double bonds. Saturated fats and oils are higher melting than unsaturated fats and oils.

SAVON DE MARSEILLE: A very mild soap unique to Provence, France. Made using ash from sea plants as the source of alkali.

SCFE: Super-critical fluid extraction. The process of extracting fragrant material (essential oils) from flowers or herbs using liquefied carbon dioxide (under high pressure).

SACCHARIDE: A sugar or carbohydrate.

SEIZE: Rapid solidification of a soap-making reaction, often forming cottage-cheese-like "globs" of soap before it can be transferred into the intended molds.

SENSITIZER: A chemical in a mixture that can cause an individual to develop allergic reactions to other materials in the same mixture.

SOAP: The sodium (or potassium) salt of a fatty acid. Soap is prepared either by the direct reaction of fatty acids with lye or by the reaction of lye with fats and oils (producing soap together with glycerin).

SORBITOL: A reduced sugar obtained by the reduction of glucose. Unlike glucose, it is relatively stable in alkaline solutions and often is used in transparent soaps to prevent crystallization, which would render the soap reflective. It also can be used in liquid soaps where again it helps prevent crystal formation.

STEARIC ACID: Fully saturated fatty acid, 18 carbon atoms in length.

STEROL: A fairly high molecular weight natural alcohol; cholesterol is the chief sterol from animals and sitosterol from vegetable sources. They are similar in composition to sebum, a natural protective "grease" in skin and hair.

SURFACTANT: A surface-active agent; the general term for a material that reduces the surface tension of water (i.e. increases the ability of water to wet a solid placed in it). Soaps and detergents are all surfactants.

SUPERFAT: Addition of excess fat or oil to the soap-making process.

SYNDET: A commercial bar "soap" containing only synthetic detergents, rather than soap.

TOCOPHEROL: Any of several natural forms of vitamin E.

TRACE: The point at which a batch of soap is thick enough to pour into molds; when it is thick enough to resist separating back into oil and water layers. Trace is the point when a spoonful of the mixture, poured back into the pot, leaves a brief, faint imprint on the surface.

TRIGLYCERIDE: A neutral compound consisting of one molecule of glycerin combined with three molecules of fatty acid. Fats and oils are triglycerides.

UNSAPONIFIABLE: Literally incapable of forming soap by saponification. Unsaponifiables primarily are tocopherols and sterols, natural emollients that soften skin.

UNSATURATION: Reactive sites in fatty acids and other organic molecules that have less than the complete amount of hydrogen. The presence of unsaturation makes oil more liquid (lowers the temperature at which it solidifies) and its soap somewhat softer. Unsaturated oils are thought to penetrate the skin and thus are often used in cosmetic creams and moisturizers.

VISCOSITY: Actually a term for resistance to flow. For example, honey is more viscous than water. An extremely viscous liquid can hardly be poured from one container to another.

WAX: An organic neutral molecule that consists of a fatty acid reacted with or attached to a fatty alcohol. Although jojoba "oil" is a wax, most waxes are solids at room temperature.

WAX ESTER: A wax compound similar in structure to a wax.

INS TABLE

FAT OR OIL	SAP for Lye (NaOH)	INS	SAP for KOH	FAT OR OIL	SAP for Lye (NaOH)	INS	SAP for KOH
almond	0.139	97	0.196	shea butter	0.128	116	0.179
apricot kernel	0.139	91	0.195	soybean	0.136	61	0.191
avocado kernel	0.133	99	0.186	sunflower seed	0.135	63	0.189
babassu	0.175	230	0.245	wheat germ	0.131	58	0.183
castor	0.129	95	0.180	carnauba wax	0.057	70	0.081
canola	0.124	56	0.174	candelilla	0.042	n/a	0.060
cocoa	0.138	157	0.194	beeswax	0.067	84	0.094
coconut	0.191	258	0.268	bison fat	0.142	170	0.199
corn	0.137	69	0.192	butterfat	0.162	191	0.227
cottonseed	0.139	89	0.194	chicken fat	0.142	130	0.199
flaxseed	0.135	-6	0.190	deer fat	0.141	166	0.197
grapeseed	0.129	66	0.181	emu fat	0.137	128	0.193
hempseed	0.137	39	0.193	goat fat	0.139	156	0.196
jojoba	0.066	11	0.092	goat butter	0.167	n/a	0.235
kukui	0.135	24	0.189	goose fat	0.137	130	0.192
linseed	0.136	12	0.190	horse fat	0.141	117	0.198
neem	0.139	124	0.195	lanolin	0.076	83	0.106
olive	0.135	109	0.190	lard	0.141	139	0.198
palm	0.142	145	0.199	mink oil	0.140	n/a	0.196
palm kernel	0.157	183	0.220	neat's foot	0.140	124	0.196
peach kernel	0.137	96	0.192	beef tallow	0.140	147	0.196
peanut	0.137	99	0.192	rabbit fat	0.143	116	0.201
safflower	0.137	47	0.192	sheep tallow	0.139	156	0.196
sesame	0.134	81	0.188	cod liver	0.128	29	0.180
shortening	0.137	115	0.192				

RESOURCES

Appalachian Valley Natural Products
260 Maple Street
Friendsville, MD 21531
Phone: 301-746-4630
Email: butchowen@av-at.com
www.AV-AT.com
Essential oils, wholesale and retail

Bear American Marketing
P.O. Box 829
Bear, DE 19701-0829
Phone: 302-836-4187
E-mail: tlshay@magpage.com
Wholesale

Bramble Berry
2138 Humboldt St.
Bellingham, WA 98225
Phone: 877-627-7883
www.brambleberry.com
Finished soap and supplies

Camden-Grey Essential Oils, Inc.
3579 N.W. 82nd Ave.
Doral, FL 33122
Phone: 866-503-8615
www.camdengrey.com
Essential oils

Columbus Foods Co.
Soapers Choice
Attn: Mike Lawson
800 North Albany
Chicago, IL 60622
Phone: 800-322-6457
Fax: 773-265-6985
www.soaperschoice.com
Most common and specialty vegetable oils

Fuji Vegetable Oil, Inc.
1 Barker Ave.
White Plains, NY 10601
Phone: 914-761-7900
Email: info@fvo-usa.com
www.fujioilusa.com
Palm and other vegetable oils

Gentle Ridge Emus
3655 Beaver Creek Drive
Hillsboro, WI 54634
Phone: 877-436-8537
Fax: 608-489-4285
Email: gentle@gentleridge.com
Emu oil

Jancas Jojoba Oil and Seed Co.
320 E. 10th Drive, Unit C
Mesa, AZ 85210
Phone: 480-497-9494
Fax: 623-321-7788
www.jancas.com
Jojoba oils and butters

The Jojoba Company
P.O. Box 586
Waldoboro, ME 04572
Phone: 800-256-5622
E-mail: hobacare@jojobacompany.com
www.jojobacompany.com
Jojoba oil, certified organic

The Lebermuth Co.
14000 McKinley Highway
Mishawaka, IN 46545
Phone: 800-648-1123
Fax: 574-258-7459
Email: info@lebermuth.com
www.lebermuth.com
Essential oils and extracts
Wholesale orders

Liberty Natural Products
20949 S. Harris Road
Oregon City, OR 97045
Phone: 800-289-8427
Fax: 503-631-2424
www.libertynatural.com
Essential and vegetable oils

Lindner Bison™ Heritage Ranch
Valencia, CA 91355
Phone: 661-254-0200
Fax: 661-254-0224
Email: klindner@lindnerbison.com
www.lindnerbison.com
Bison soap, and bison food products

Majestic Mountain Sage
918 West 700 North Ste. 104
Logan, Utah 84321
Phone: 435-755-0863
Fax: 435-755-2108
www.thesage.com
Online lye calculator, essential and
fragrance oils and supplies

Milky Way Molds
PMB No. 473
4326 S.E. Woodstock
Portland, OR 97206
Phone: 503-774-4157
www.milkywaymolds.com
Individual soap molds and books

Nashville Wraps
242 Molly Walton Drive
Hendersonville, TN 37075
Phone: 800-547-9727
www.nashvillewraps.com
Wrapping supplies of all types, catalog
available

Nature's Gift
316 Old Hickory Blvd. East
Madison, TN 37115
Phone: 615-612-4270
Fax: 615-860-9171
www.naturesgift.com
Essential oils

Natural Sourcing, LLC
341 Christian Street
Oxford, CT 06478
Phone: 800-340-0080
www.naturalsourcing.com
Soap base, essential oils, supplies

Pilot Chemical Company
2744 E. Kemper Road
Cincinnati, OH 45341
Phone: 513-326-0600
Fax: 513-326-601
www.pilotchemical.com
Personal care surfactants

Rainbow Meadow
4494 Brooklyn Rd.
Jackson, MI 49201
Phone: 800-207-4047
Fax: 517-764-9766
www.rainbowmeadow.com
Essential oils and soap supplies

Saponifier Magazine
P.O. Box 280
Silvana, WA 98287
Phone: 425-760-1004
Email: saponifier@gmail.com
www.saponifier.com
The Saponifier, bimonthly trade magazine for soap and toiletry makers

Soap Crafters, Inc.
6255 McLeod Drive, Suite 15
Las Vegas, NV 89120
Phone: 877-484-5121
Fax: 888-782-0160
www.soapcrafters.com
Full range of soap supplies

SKS Bottle & Packaging
2600 7th Ave.
Building 60 West
Watervliet, NY 12189
Phone: 518-880-6980 ext. 1
Fax: 518-880-6990
www.sks-bottle.com
Wide range of bottles, vials, and jars

Snowdrift Farm
2750 South 4th Avenue
Suites 107 & 108
Tucson, Arizona 85713
Phone: 888-999-6950
Fax: 520-882-2739
www.snowdriftfarm.com
Soap bases, fragrances and more

Stepan Company - United States
22 W. Frontage Road
Northfield, IL 60093
Phone: 847-446-7500
Fax: 847-501-2100
www.stepan.com/en
Personal care surfactants

Sunburst Bottle Co.
4500 Beloit Drive
Sacramento, CA 95838
Phone: 916-929-4500
Fax: 916-929-3604
www.sunburstbottle.com
Bottles and jars

The Boyer Corporation
9600 East Ogden Avenue
La Grange, IL 60525
Phone: 708-352-2553
www.boyercorporation.com
Lye for soap makers

The Chemistry Store.com
1133 Walter Price St.
Cayce, SC 29033
Phone: 800-224-1430
Fax: 803-926-5389
Email: sales@chemistrystore.com
www.chemistrystore.com
Soap making supplies

TKB Trading LLC
1101 9th Ave.
Oakland, CA 94606
Phone: 510-451-9011
Fax: 510-451-4377
Email: tkb_shipping@yahoo.com
www.tkbtrading.com
Soap bases, colorants

Wholesale Supplies Plus
10035 Broadview Rd.
Broadview Heights, OH 44147
Phone: 800-359-0944
Fax: 440-526-6597
www.wholesalesuppliesplus.com
Wide variety of soap supplies

BIBLIOGRAPHY

Booth, Nancy M. "Scentsations: A Handbook for Fragrance Crafting." 1995.

Bramsom, Ann. "Soap: Making It, Enjoying It." 2nd ed. New York: Workman Publishing Co., 1975.

Buchanan, Rita, ed. "Taylor's Guide to Herbs." New York: Houghton Mifflin Co., 1995.

Cavitch, Susan Miller. "The Natural Soap Book: Making Herbal and Vegetable-Based Soaps." Pownal: Storey Publishing, 1995.

Drury, Susan. "Tea Tree Oil, A Medicine Kit in a Bottle." Essex: C.W. Daniel Company, Ltd., 1992.

Eckroth, D. ed. "Kirk-Othmer Concise Encyclopedia of Chemical Technology." New York: Wiley-Interscience, John Wiley & Sons, Inc., 1985.

Genders, Roy. "The Complete Book of Herbs and Herb Growing." New York: Sterling Publishing Co., 1982.

Hayes, Alan. "Bath Scents." New York: Angus & Robertson, 1994.

Hui, Y. H. ed. "Bailey's Industrial Oil & Fat Products." 5th ed. New York: Wiley-Interscience, John Wiley & Sons, Inc., 1996.

Lawless, Julia. "The Illustrated Encyclopedia of Essential Oils." 2nd edition. Element Books Ltd., 1995.

---. "The Complete Guide to the Use of Oils in Aromatherapy and Herbalism." Rockport: Element Books, 1995.

Maine, Sandy. "The Soap Book: Simple Herbal Recipes." Loveland: Interweave Press, Inc., 1995.

Mills, Simon Y. "The Essential Book of Herbal Medicine." New York: Penguin Books, 1993.

Rose, Jeanne. "The Aromatherapy Book: Applications & Inhalations." Herbal Studies Course. Berkeley: Jeanne Rose and North Atlantic Books, 1992.

Ryman, Daniele. "Aromatherapy: The Complete Guide to Plant and Flower Essences for Health and Beauty." New York: Bantam, 1993.

Sellar, Wanda. "The Directory of Essential Oils." Essex: C.W. Daniel Company, Ltd., 1992.

Stuart, Malcolm, ed. "The Encyclopedia of Herbs and Herbalism." London: Orbis Publishing, 1979.

Valnet, Jean, M.D. "The Practice of Aromatherapy." Rochester: Healing Arts Press, 1990.

Webb, David A. "Making Potpourri Colognes and Soaps." Summit: Tab Books, 1988.

White, Elaine C. "Soap Recipes: Seventy Tried-and-True Ways to Make Modern Soap with Herbs, Beeswax, and Vegetable Oils." Starkville: Valley Hills Press, 1995.

Windholz, M., ed. "The Merck Index," 9th ed. Rahway: Merck & Co. Inc., 1976.

INDEX

METRIC TABLES

WEIGHT (OR MASS)

IMPERIAL UNIT	METRIC UNIT	METRIC UNIT	IMPERIAL UNIT
Ounce	28.35 grams	Gram	0.035 ounces
Pound	0.45 kilograms	Kilogram	2.21 pounds
UK ton (2240 pounds)	1.02 metric tons	Metric ton (1000kg)	0.98 UK tons
US ton (2000 pounds)	0.91 tons	Metric ton (1000kg)	1.10 US tons

VOLUME

IMPERIAL UNIT	METRIC UNIT	METRIC UNIT	IMPERIAL UNIT
Teaspoon (UK)	5.92 milliliters	Milliliter	0.17 teaspoons (UK)
Teaspoon (US)	4.93 milliliters	Milliliter	0.20 teaspoons (US)
Tablespoon (UK)	17.76 milliliters	10 Milliliter	0.56 tablespoons (UK)
Tablespoon (US)	14.79 milliliters	10 Milliliter	0.68 tablespoons (US)
Fluid ounce (UK)	28.41 milliliters	100 Milliliter	3.52 fluid ounces (UK)
Fluid ounce (US)	29.57 milliliters	100 Milliliter	3.38 fluid ounces (US)
Pint (UK)	0.57 liters	Liter	1.76 pints (UK)
Pint (US)	0.47 liters	Liter	2.11 pints (US)
Quart (UK)	1.14 liters	Liter	0.88 quarts (UK)
Quart (US)	0.95 liters	Liter	1.06 quarts (US)
Gallon (UK)	4.55 liters	Liter	0.22 gallon (UK)
Gallon (US)	3.79 liters	Liter	0.26 gallon (US)

METRIC CONVERSION CHART

TO CALCULATE:	MULTIPLY:	BY:
Ounces into grams	28	Number of ounces
Grams into ounces	0.035	Number of grams
Pounds into kilograms	0.45	Number of pounds
Kilograms into pounds	2.2	Number of kilograms
Teaspoons into milliliters	5	Number of teaspoons
Tablespoons into milliliters	15	Number of tablespoons
Fluid ounces into milliliters	30	Number of fluid ounces
Milliliters into fluid ounces	0.034	Number of milliliters
Cups into liters	0.24	Number of cups
Pints into liters	0.47	Number of pints
Quarts into liters	0.95	Number of pints

TEMPERATURE

$C = (F - 32) \div 1.8$	For example: $(68 F - 32) \div 1.8 = (36) \div 1.8 = 20 C$
$F = (C \times 1.8) + 32$	For example: $(20 C \times 1.8) + 32 = (36) + 32 = 68 F$

ABOUT THE AUTHORS

Dr. Robert McDaniel received a Bachelor of Science degree in chemistry from the University of Notre Dame and a doctorate in organic chemistry from the University of Missouri – Rolla. After two years as a postdoctoral fellow at the University of Chicago, he began his industrial career in the surfactant industry developing the active ingredients that go into household detergents and fabric softeners. For the next 20 years he worked at the bench and as a manager developing a variety of surfactants.

Dr. McDaniel now teaches various science courses at the high school and community college level in Southern California. He also writes a column for the Saponifier online magazine, which targets professionals (and talented amateurs) in the soap- and candle-making industries. Oh yes, and in his copious spare time, he makes soap under contract, acts as a consultant to small soap-making businesses, and he is the author of 20 U.S. Patents and numerous European patents.

Katherine (Katie) McDaniel is the artistic and creative heart of the couple. She is a weaver, fiber artist, chandler, photographer (supplied the bulk of photographs used in both "Essentially Soap" and "Essentially Candles"), hot glass artist, goldsmith and metal worker. She "encouraged" her husband to enter the soap-making field when he began to be overly helpful in her fine American craft business. Over the years, she has taught weaving, spinning and jewelry making. In her copious spare time she is a community activist.

The McDaniels first soap-making book, "Essentially Soap," has sold over 33,000 copies worldwide. They have one son and grandson (Benjamin and Darien respectively.) Ben is a jeweler in Maine and Darien is, of course, absolutely wonderful. The McDaniels live in Laguna Woods, California.

More Ways to Simplify and Save

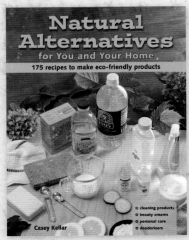

This easy-to-follow guide is unlike any "recipe book" you've seen. Inside you'll find 175 recipes for everything from bath soaps and ointments to window cleaners, insect repellents and potting soil. All of the ingredients are affordable, every day items, and in addition to the recipes you'll find tips and hints for simplifying your life, 300+ inspiring photographs, and cost savings counters to show you what you'll save by making your own products.

Softcover, 208 p
Item# Z4649 • $24.99

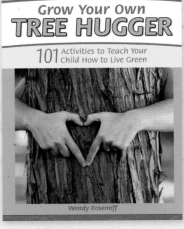

This fun and colorful book offers a wonderful array of projects to teach children from pre-school to high school the essentials about protecting our earth. Inside you'll find 101 projects like growing seeds using old sponges, learning about the impact of global warming through, creating a homemade pizza with home-grown herbs and much more.

Softcover, 240 p
Item# Z4974 • $19.99

From simple bath soaps to beautiful aromatic bars you can give as gifts, this guide from the popular *Everything* series leads you through the process, from start to finish. You'll learn where to look for the necessary ingredients and equipment, how to experiment with different solutions to create everything from kitchen cleaning soap to facial soap.

Softcover, 320 p
Item# 229-1 • $15.95

Bid farewell to foods filled with unhealthy ingredients and empty calories and stop spending more than you need to when you turn to this book and its 225 affordable make-ahead mixes. With this book in hand you'll have a pantry shelf full of dry and liquid mixes you can use to master muffins, spice up your favorite salads, create wholesome and delicious soups, develop delicious rubs for any type of meat, and treat your family and friends to refreshing drinks.

Softcover, 240 p
Item# Z5032 • $19.99